Advance Praise For
American Wheels, Chinese Roads
The Story of General Motors in China

I've shared many experiences with Michael Dunne on the front lines of China, and Michael knows China and the automobile market unlike anyone else I've met. His personal adventures and experiences give him a brilliant insight into an American icon's journey into China. He chronicles it with intrigue, analysis, drama and humor. You can't put it down!

James D. Power IV
Former Executive at J.D. Power and Associates and
Co-author of Satisfaction: How Every Great Company
Listens to the Voice of the Customer

Michael Dunne has done a superb job of chronicling and analyzing the very important and complex business story of GM in China. He has done this based on his "boots on the ground" experience of many years in Middle Kingdom and his great depth of understanding of the global auto industry. As we increase the speed of globalization, it is imperative to understand the many complex issues involved from the importance of personal relationships to understanding diverse cultures to even have a chance for success. The deep insight into the high stakes drama in the GM–China story reaches well beyond the auto industry and, perhaps, well beyond China. Consequently this is a must-read for all who are involved in global commercial activities.

David Cole
Chairman Emeritus, Center for Automotive Research

American Wheels, Chinese Roads is a fascinating portrait of GM's rocky road to success in China. Author Michael Dunne takes you on a wild ride, chronicling the failures, the successes, and the sheer random luck of an American company trying to seal the deal with the Chinese. Dunne's access is unprecedented, his sources second-to-none. This is a book not only about the transformation of an American icon, but about China, revealed in all its complicated beauty.

Rob Schmitz
China Bureau Chief, Marketplace/American Public Media

AMERICAN WHEELS
CHINESE ROADS

The Story of General Motors in China

AMERICAN WHEELS

CHINESE ROADS

The Story of General Motors in China

Michael J. Dunne

WILEY
John Wiley & Sons (Asia) Pte. Ltd.

Other Wiley Editorial Offices
John Wiley & Sons, 111 River Street, Hoboken, NJ 07030, USA
John Wiley & Sons, The Atrium, Southern Gate, Chichester, West Sussex, P019 8SQ,
    United Kingdom
John Wiley & Sons (Canada) Ltd., 5353 Dundas Street West, Suite 400, Toronto,
    Ontario, M9B 6HB, Canada
John Wiley & Sons Australia Ltd., 42 McDougall Street, Milton, Queensland 4064,
    Australia
Wiley-VCH, Boschstrasse 12, D-69469 Weinheim, Germany

Library of Congress Cataloging-in-Publication Data
ISBN 978–0–470–82861–8 (Hardcover)
ISBN 978–0–470–82864–9 (ePDF)
ISBN 978–0–470–82862–5 (Mobi)
ISBN 978–0–470–82865–6 (ePub)

Typeset in 11/14 Sabon Roman by MPS Limited, a Macmillan Company
Printed in Singapore by Markono Print Media Pte. Ltd.

10 9 8 7 6 5 4 3 2 1

I dedicate this book to my parents: Janet for the lilt of her Irish laughter. And Jim, for inspiring the pursuit of a road less traveled.

CONTENTS

ACKNOWLEDGMENTS

I was making my way up six flights of concrete stairs to our Shanghai apartment in the old French Quarter one evening in 2005, briefcase in one hand and Chinese grocery bags slipping from the other, when the thought first came to me: *there must be a story here.* It wasn't until 2009, though, that I was ready to turn my twenty years of experiences in China into a book.

But how? I had already developed an expertise in China's car market through my company, Automotive Resources Asia. Could there be a connection between my first-hand experiences in China and the car business? No, China was China and cars were cars. Two entirely different subjects. The book idea got stuck.

That's when other people started to make things happen.

First came this simple advice from my father, Jim Dunne: "Write it down." And so I started to record little episodes, the telling details, even though I had no idea what the book would be about. It continued that way for months, until—after a morning coffee meet in Singapore—Sylvia McKaige of CNBC introduced me to Wiley Asia. Nick Melchior at Wiley worked with me to channel my stack of notes into a business book about GM in China.

I was off and running.

Well, not so fast. It is one thing to want to tell what you saw. It is quite another to do it in a way that makes the reader want more. Editors Chris Endres, Kristi Hein, and Debbie Mettenleiter suggested adjustments that improved clarity and flow in huge ways.

General Motors helpfully arranged site visits and many key interviews. Scores of other industry executives, many of whom wish to remain anonymous, contributed invaluable first-hand accounts.

That little devil called "doubt" has a way of slipping uninvited into a writer's lair from time to time. When that happened, the following talented people stepped in to deliver shots of encouragement and solid advice: John Bonnell, David Collins, Patrick Cranley, Timothy Dunne, Lauren Giglio, Paul Ingrassia, Kerry Ivan, Tina Kanagaratnam, Marian Knappert, Linda Lim, Jane Lanhee Lee, Paul Lienert, Mark Leonard, Geoff Liu, Richard McGregor, Jerry Powers, Frank Rocco, Matthew Schroeder, Paul Stepanek Frances Bauer, Julie Dunne, Patricia Dunne, and Mary Jo Finkenstaedt.

During the journey of my giving life to this book, my wife, Merlien, gave birth to our second child Aurelia *and then to our third child*, Connor. In a blink of time, our three-year old, Raphael, was joined by a sister and brother.

I am forever grateful to Merlien for being an ocean of serenity in the midst of a beautiful storm of chaos at home.

INTRODUCTION

Taking the first step is so sublime, so enthralling, so utterly enticing that no businessman can resist. The tree-lined, flower-petaled path lures you, like a moth to the light, to the shining entrance of the world's most promising marketplace: China.

As you approach the gates and prepare to pass through into this lucrative and boundless market, you discover that they are locked. Never mind looking for a key. These forbidding gates can be opened only from the inside. You must be invited to enter. And then you may proceed only in the company of a chaperone. This isn't a dream sequence. This is the reality of doing business in China.

General Motors found itself in just this position in the early 1990s. It wanted to "open up" the China market, but found that the doors were shut tight. Government officials in Beijing had already issued joint venture car production licenses to a handful of companies, including Chrysler and Volkswagen.

But GM had to wait. And wait some more.

As a student intern at GM headquarters in Detroit in the summer of 1989, I witnessed the waiting period firsthand. I was assigned to devise a distribution strategy for China just in case, one day, China decided to invite GM inside.

GM's own "culture" was crystallized for me in one unforgettable moment when I was preparing a presentation to the higher-ups at the end of my eight-week tenure. My supervisor walked through the report and then offered only one piece of advice: "Whatever you do, just make sure to C-Y-A."

"'C-Y-A'?"

"Cover your ass. The bosses will know little about China," he explained, "but that won't stop them from calling you out, just to show they know something about Asia."

I had little to fear about covering anything. I was born and raised in Detroit, I'd had behind-the-wheel access to every new car in America sold during the previous nine years, and I'd taught and studied in Chongqing's Institute of Architecture and Engineering for a year before coming to GM.

China at the time was still a tiny car market, with annual sales less than that of the state of Michigan. The Chongqing university where I studied, home to fifteen thousand people, owned a grand total of one car—the Red Flag, a ponderous four-door sedan based on the 1955 Chrysler Imperial.

But the small demand for cars did nothing to deter the appetite for stamping a footprint in the biggest potential market in Asia, a pressing hunger easily fueled by imagination: *With all those people, just think how giant China's car market could one day be! We could make a killing just selling hubcaps!*

Even über optimists, however, could not have imagined that twenty years later, China would be the world's number one car market, handily surpassing the United States. And no one inside GM could have dreamt that in 2010 the company would sell one million cars—Chevys, Buicks, and Cadillacs—to Chinese customers.

Once GM secured passage through the front gates into the Middle Kingdom, the company almost immediately discovered that China is a tough and unpredictable place to do business. For every delicious opportunity to make a fortune, there is an equally dangerous pitfall. For every promise kept, there is a promise broken. And there are shifting government rules at every turn.

The untold story is that GM's road to success in China has never been straight or easy. The company waited long years just to get permission to build passenger cars in China. It was not until 1999 that Shanghai GM started production of its first model, the Buick Century. GM has prevailed thanks to gutsy leadership, perseverance, and, yes, some good old-fashioned luck.

Never before in the history of the automobile has the industry seen growth as explosive as it's been in China. That's where the luck came in. Annual demand for new cars has rocketed from six hundred forty thousand cars in 2000 to more than eleven million in 2010. GM's operations with its Chinese partners today generate billions of dollars of revenues and hundreds of millions of dollars in profits.

GM's success in China stands in sharp contrast to the failures in North America and Europe that led the company into bankruptcy in 2009. The fact that GM in China could triumph while its parent company was self-destructing is both remarkable and revealing.

And yet, there remains a certain fragility to GM's success in China. Buick, Cadillac, and Chevrolet must compete for market share against fifty other marques—Toyota, Honda, Hyundai, Volkswagen, and other industry powerhouses. And GM is vulnerable to unexpected regulations decreed by powerful government officials in Beijing. The path to financial nirvana remains neither straight or certain.

This is the story of how GM got into China, what it confronted, and how it tackled the formidable challenges presented by the Middle Kingdom—an arena of competition entirely different from America. The hard lessons learned will be instructive not just to companies making cars, but to any foreign company with aspirations to make it in China—an enormous market that will remain highly unsettled, and unsettling.

Part One

Rules of the Chinese Road

I

SCALING NEW HEIGHTS

The producers of *60 Minutes* had unearthed a story, and they wanted the inside scoop: How had General Motors managed to compete—indeed, to *thrive*—in China, while the rest of the company declined into the shameful bankruptcy of 2009? They put this question to GM executives in China and Detroit during the summer of 2010. But GM wasn't talking, so the program was shelved.

That's too bad, because *60 Minutes* viewers missed the opportunity to hear a good story. Not a fairy-tale story with a happy ending for all, but a story that would bring to life the strange and unfamiliar rules of the road that make doing business in China a very uncertain endeavor.

If you gauge China accurately and have a little luck, you make a fortune. Get it wrong, and there will be no good Samaritans to help you out of the roadside ditch. For GM, there were many potholes, detours, U-turns, setbacks, surprises, and disappointments before any money was made.

If the executives had spoken on camera, viewers would no doubt have heard a litany of the traditional factors of success: product, pricing, positioning, and placement. Those are all important, of course. But they do not get to the heart of how competition works in China. To understand how GM—or any company—flourishes in China, you must begin with a look at the very different nature of that competition. In China, everything begins with a license.

You don't just walk into China and start selling Buicks and Chevys and Cadillacs. You need a license to build cars. You need a license to sell cars. You need a license to import product.

You need a license to export product. You need a license to turn your Chinese yuan into U.S. dollars. You need a license to do just about anything that involves money—which is to say you need a license to do most things in today's China.

Even small businesses are closely regulated. Any foreign company that opens a subsidiary in Shanghai must make a minimum $140,000 initial capital contribution. It's a rule. Once the money reaches a Chinese bank, it stays there. If one month later, you have a change of heart and want to move your money back out, well, you can't. It remains in China until your firm is formally closed, which could take a year or more. Maybe there will be an audit, which will push the timeline out even further.

Frank Rocco, a street-smart attorney with nine years in Shanghai, distills the rules around money flows. "China makes it very easy for the money to come in, and very difficult for you to move it back out." And even after money enters a bank account inside China, you still need to get approval for a business license.

To get a license in the car industry, you need a Chinese partner. It's the law. If you find a partner and if the government approves of the partnership, then the partner can help you get the license. Foreign car companies building and selling cars in China all have partners. And all of the Chinese partners have no less than a 50-percent ownership stake in the joint venture. That's a regulation, too.

In the car industry, the domestic partner is usually a major municipality like Shanghai, Beijing, Guangzhou, or even the central government itself. Some licenses are issued by the city, your partner. Other licenses are approved and issued by the central government. It's complicated, to be sure.

China protects its auto industry, citing national security as its primary reason, so some licensing is understandable. But the strict culture of licensing does not stop at cars. The Chinese government has its hands in almost every aspect of the economy, often to the unending frustration of foreign companies trying to penetrate this gigantic marketplace.

You can get a feel for how the licensing system shapes business in China only by going there. After your flight lands at the Shanghai Pudong International Airport, you make your way past the giant floor-to-ceiling advertisements for DHL, MasterCard, and Bank of China. You likely will be struck by how brightly lit, modern, and clean this massive airport really is.

You work your way through a dense river of people in the arrival hall and step outside into the thick Shanghai air, to the curbside taxi stand. This is the point where you really enter China, where you first notice how licenses define the commercial landscape.

As you'd expect, the taxis are a myriad of colors—red, white, burnt orange, light green, blue, and turquoise, each representing a different company. But the make and model never vary. Without exception, every taxi is a Volkswagen Santana; an aged model built in Shanghai without interruption since 1984. The Santana is an inexpensive, utilitarian machine that moves reliably from point A to point B. That pretty much exhausts the car's strong points.

Invariably, you have to tug on the door handle a couple of times before the latch succumbs and allows the back door to open. Once inside, you'll note the seats are completely inadequate, the clutch squeaks, wind noise invades through the loose window seals, and the air conditioning never quite makes it to the back seat. The aging Santana taxis' mechanicals and plain styling are an odd juxtaposition to the twenty-first-century airport. That's to say nothing of the surfeit of refined, luxury autos—Audis, Cadillacs, Mercedes, and BMW X-5s—you can see rolling in and out of the airport parking lot across the street.

So how is it that this wealthy city, the leading light of China's march to capitalism, the trend-setter of Chinese fashion and bling, permits the aging and clunky Santana to monopolize the city's fleet of taxis?

It comes down to money, of course. It cannot be overstated that in China, every channel to money has a license attached to it. A permit. Permission to enter the market.

There are forty-five thousand Santana taxis coursing through the streets of Shanghai. Most of them belong to one of a handful of state-owned enterprises, the largest of which is DaZhong, which means "the masses." Dazong's taxis are all painted turquoise.

The story of Shanghai's leading taxi service, DaZhong Taxi, tells us much about the way China works. It also provides insight into how GM competes in China. Formed in 1988, the Shanghai DaZhong Taxi Company was one of the first companies to list on the Shanghai Stock Exchange in 1992. "That's the most important difference," explains a driver from a competing, orange-painted taxi, referring to the success of DaZhong. "They got approval to list [on the stock exchange], which gives them more money. They take that money to advertise. They got permission to list and we did not."

Yang Guoping cofounded Shanghai Dazhong. In 2000, CEO Yang was selected as a "national model worker," a prize bestowed by the Chinese Communist Party upon the best workers in the nation. Five years later, the Party selected Yang as one of the "Top-10 Individuals with Outstanding Quality Achievements in China." Out of 1.4 billion people, Yang was selected as one of the ten best businessmen.

Like many other successful businesspeople in China today, the fifty-five-year-old Mr. Yang has been both an active member of the Young Entrepreneurs Association and a loyal member of the Communist Party. These seemingly at-odds affiliations are the result of a half-reformed society that is partly command economy (one in which the government regulates supplies and prices) and partly unbridled capitalism. Or, more accurately, it is unfettered capitalism within the arbitrary bounds outlined by the Party and its government officials.

Back in 1998, then Chinese Premier Zhu Rongji, formerly mayor of Shanghai, wrote an inscription to mark the company's tenth birthday: "It is arduous and hard to create a business and it is a long way to scale new heights." A long way to scale new heights becomes a little shorter when you understand where to buy your taxis.

"They have the right to buy any car," explained the driver of the orange-colored taxi."But they don't exercise that right, you see?"

It is not a matter of limited choice. Today there are more than sixty different car brands on offer in China. There are more car brands produced in China than in any other market in the world, including the United States. There's Mercedes, Audi, BMW, and Volkswagen from Germany; Ford and GM from America; Hyundai and Kia from Korea; and Toyota, Nissan, Mazda, Honda, and Suzuki from Japan. Even the French (Peugeot and Citroën) and the Italian (Fiat)—companies that do not compete in the United States— are now in the Chinese game. The Chinese car marketplace is further enriched by more than two dozen Chinese car brands, led by names like Geely, Chery, Great Wall, Brilliance, and BYD.

Indeed, Mr. Yang could buy cars from anywhere. But he always buys his cars—his *Santanas*—from Shanghai Volkswagen, the

Chinese-German joint venture. He does this primarily because doing so provides a kind of insurance policy. So long as DaZhong buys Shanghai Volkswagen Santanas, there is a good chance that its license to manage the city's largest fleet of nearly nine thousand taxis will be renewed by city authorities. Yes, DaZhong buys its taxis from the same place it gets its business license.

Every time DaZhong Taxi Company buys or services a Santana, the City of Shanghai takes half the revenue. That is because the City of Shanghai also happens to own the Shanghai Automotive Industry Corporation (SAIC). This massive state enterprise achieved $25 billion in revenues in 2008. That was enough to place it at number 359 in the *Fortune* 500 in 2009.

SAIC runs two giant car joint ventures—Shanghai General Motors and Shanghai Volkswagen—that together employ tens of thousands of people. Shanghai GM is situated on the eastern side of the Huangpu River in an area known as Pudong. Shanghai VW makes camp on the western side of the river, or Puxi, where it produces the Santanas. There's actually a third major player here, too: the City of Shanghai also makes and markets its own brand of sedans under its Roewe brand name.

In 2010, Shanghai GM and Shanghai VW produced two million cars. All of the taxis and a large percentage of the cars seen tooling on the roads in Shanghai are made by these companies, with half of the ownership belonging to the city. The Buick Regals and Excelles, Chevrolet Cruzes and Volkswagen Passats, Tiguans, and Polos come from the Shanghai GM and Shanghai Volkswagen joint ventures.

Like all foreign automakers wishing to build and sell cars in China, GM was required to form a joint venture with a Chinese partner. That is the law. Ninety-five percent of cars sold in China are produced in China, because steep taxes make imports extremely expensive. The joint venture gives GM and VW access to a license that allows them to build and sell cars. No joint venture, no car factory, and no chance at selling in the world's largest automotive market. With the joint venture, GM has anted up for a license and will be dealt some cards and some room in which to play them.

The commercial goal of selling more GM Buicks and Chevrolets in China becomes a political and economic campaign to enhance the power and might of the city of Shanghai. Think of it as Shanghai, Inc., with the mayor as chairman and CEO.

It is in this complex competitive arena that GM has found its way to incredibly strong growth and profits. In 2010, GM and its Chinese partners built more than one million Buicks, Chevrolets and Cadillacs and generated close to $1 billion in profits. GM splits the revenue and profits with the City of Shanghai.

In a front-page article that ran in July 2010, the *New York Times* captured the success story.

> As G.M. prepares a public stock offering later this year, China is emerging as a crucial piece of its appeal to potential investors. In the first half of this year, G.M.'s China sales rose 48.5 percent over the same period last year, and for the first time ever, the automaker sold more vehicles in China than in the United States. Just 13 years after entering China, G.M. now says the country accounts for a quarter of its global sales.

Why would GM executives not want to share this success story with *60 Minutes* in advance of the IPO? One possibility is that a close look at China would embarrass people in charge of GM's woeful operations in the United States and Europe.

But a more likely reason is that, sooner or later, the investigative reporters at *60 Minutes* would come across a startling fact: GM's success in China depends heavily on the goodwill of its partner, SAIC, which, of course, is owned by the City of Shanghai. The Shanghai municipal government, in turn, is part of the Chinese government. The officials at all levels of the government ultimately report to the Chinese Communist Party. The difficulty, then, is how to explain to American viewers—the taxpayers who owned 66 percent of the company in 2010—that one vital ingredient in GM's success is its implicit alignment with the Chinese Communist Party?

To enter and compete in China, you need a license. To get a license you need a friend. Once you have a license, that friend can help you build your business. The better the friendship, the more lucrative the business. If the friendship ever turns sour, the business will be in trouble. Your friend might ultimately aim to control your business.

"It is arduous and hard to create a business and it is a long way to scale new heights" said former Premier Zhu Rongji, who proved instrumental in helping GM secure a license in China to make cars.

GM had to travel a long hard road before it scaled new heights in China.

2

MANY DETROITS

If central government planning officials in Beijing had their way, Shanghai would be one of only a handful of automotive manufacturing centers in China. The officials believe that China's automotive strength must arise from concentration and consolidation of people, assets, and production volumes, just as it has in America, Germany, Japan, and Korea.

But that's not been the case. In today's China, where power has devolved to the cities, every mayor wants a piece of the automotive action—it means more jobs and a larger tax base in their own backyard. As the total market for cars and trucks approaches twenty million vehicles a year, everyone wants in. As a result, there are many, many "Detroits of China."

Leading Chinese cities like Beijing, Guangzhou, Wuhan, and Chongqing have developed massive automotive industrial complexes that each employ tens of thousands of people. They partner with foreign automakers to access products and manufacturing technologies. Think of powerful municipalities as the hubs of the automotive industry; foreign joint ventures are the spokes.

In Beijing, for example, the state-owned Beijing Automotive Industry Corp. has ownership in separate 50–50 joint ventures with Hyundai and Mercedes. And it will be building its own brand of cars, Beijing, starting in 2011. Guangzhou partners with Toyota and Honda in two separate joint ventures and will add Fiat and Mitsubishi joint ventures in the future. Guangzhou has announced plans for its own brand, called the Everus.

Altogether, there are now six major "Detroits of China" and many minor ones. They are scattered in all regions of the country, from the frigid north to the tropical south, like errant darts on a board. Their existence owes more to the outcomes of political friendships along the way than to any master plan. Each aims to be crowned number one in China. Competition among the cities—and even within the cities—is ruthless, as each seeks dominance over the others. The City of Shanghai makes the most cars today, but the other cities are not far behind.

To begin to understand the Chinese auto industry, think about it like this: Imagine the City of Detroit forming two 50–50 joint ventures, one with Toyota on the east side of town and a separate one with Honda on the west side, while also producing cars under its own brand name: Detroit Motors. The mayor of Detroit would appoint one of his officials to be the chairman of Detroit Motors, and that chairman would select the presidents for one of the joint ventures.

Continuing the scenario, City of Detroit officials working at the Detroit-Honda joint venture this year may be unexpectedly seconded to the Detroit-Toyota joint venture next year. To illustrate this, the current president of Shanghai Automotive Industry Corp. worked first for Shanghai Volkswagen, then later for Shanghai GM, before ascending to the presidency at SAIC. People come and go between ventures, just like that.

Global automakers—companies that are used to dictating terms to their suppliers and securing special deals from state government back home—find themselves in the vulnerable position of visitors to China's giant, state-guided vehicle manufacturing enterprises. "Some days it feels like we're just like concubines," is how one western automotive executive summed it up.

Even the order of names in the joint venture companies is revealing: the Chinese name always comes first, even though the partnerships feature a 50–50 share structure. It is always Guangzhou-Toyota, never Toyota-Guangzhou. It is always Beijing-Hyundai, never Hyundai-Beijing; always Shanghai-Volkswagen, never Volkswagen-Shanghai. This ordering of names is particularly significant in China, where hierarchy—who comes first—is the basis of social interaction and, by extension, power in the marketplace.

Chinese consumers play a role in shaping the industry, too. We know that Japanese consumers buy Japanese cars and Koreans buy Korean cars. Consumers in those two countries choose homegrown brands because of nationalism, trade barriers, and recognition of the quality of the vehicles. In China, things are a little different:

The market is dominated not by Chinese cars but by foreign brands in 50–50 joint ventures with Chinese cities. Chinese consumers, unlike the Koreans and the Japanese, demonstrate no discernable loyalty to Chinese brands. In fact, the majority of Chinese car buyers hold most Chinese car brands in disdain, at least so far. Foreign brands comprise 70 percent of China's car market, or around seven and a half million cars in 2010.

The car-building Chinese cities act almost like sovereign countries, building a fortress around their home markets, while working very hard to "export" their cars to other Chinese cities. Travel to Beijing and the taxi fleet is dominated by Hyundai Elantras, produced by the Beijing-Hyundai joint venture. Make your way to Wuhan and the taxi fleets are full of Citroëns, made in—where else?—the city of Wuhan.

There's one more twist: Chinese partners in the joint ventures each have ambitions to design and develop their own cars. SAIC builds cars under its own brand name—Roewe. For cities like Shanghai, this makes foreign car companies like Volkswagen and General Motors today's partner and, inevitably, tomorrow's adversary. But the line between today and tomorrow is hazy.

Once you understand this competitive territory and its rules, it quickly becomes apparent that the fate of any foreign car company in China is bound tightly (and quite awkwardly) to the political and financial clout of its Chinese partner—the local or central government. And so Shanghai GM finds itself competing against cross-town rival, Shanghai Volkswagen, against the Shanghai Automotive Industry Corporation (with its Roewe) and against other joint venture companies across the country.

This is hardly an environment conducive to trust. And when trust breaks down, joint ventures crumble like sand castles before an incoming tide. Of the three initial joint ventures blessed by the central government in the mid-1980s, one, Shanghai Volkswagen, muscled its way to market dominance. A second, Guangzhou-Peugeot, was on its way to bankruptcy. And another, Beijing Jeep, was rife with animosity and deception. The main source of dissension: determining which side gets to keep the money.

GM in the early 1990s was not yet thinking about how to split the money. It was still searching for a way inside.

3

GETTING A FOOTHOLD—
IN QUICKSAND

Business in China is a bit like a Las Vegas casino or the New York Stock Exchange. Players' actions are driven, alternately, by greed and fear. The gut might say *Stay away,* but the eyes see other people making so much money that temptation prevails. When you do decide to play, you're not entirely sure of the risks or the upside.

China lets you decide whether you want to enter or not. For many years, GM could not make up its mind.

The Beijing Auto Show was the backdrop for an episode that perfectly illustrates the dilemma faced by many companies with a yen for China. On a sweltering evening in June—the opening day of the show—senior executives from the British design engineering industry had to make a choice. Would they leave for dinner, after standing outdoors in Beijing's thick heat and humidity all afternoon dressed in suits and ties, or would they stay put and hope for a visit from the Chinese minister of industry?

The show officials had just stopped by the British stand to explain some rules: All delegates were free to go at any time. But if you chose to leave after 5:30 P.M., reentry would not be permitted. You could leave, but there would be no getting back into the show—whether you had passes or not. And if you left, you might miss a visit from the minister.

China made no secret of its quest to build its own cars, powered by its own engines. Meeting the minister of industry in person at the Beijing Auto Show just might help to accelerate British engineering business growth in China.

On the other hand, the senior executives were jet-lagged, hot, and hungry.

After some deliberation, the British decided to stay. Six o'clock came and went, as did seven, without any sign of the minister. By eight o'clock, the summer dusk was turning to darkness. Growing restless, the British looked up and down the aisles to see what executives from other delegations were doing. They felt a little better when they saw people from Honda and Nissan still manning their respective stages. No one dared to leave early, it seemed.

By 8:30, however, some of the executives were annoyed. They summoned the organizers of the show for an explanation. "Was the minister coming after all—or not?" they asked.

The official disappeared into the darkness and after several minutes came back with an answer: "The minister did not say that he was not coming."

"Pardon me," said one of the British executives, "but what does that mean?" The unspoken question: *Is that "Yes, he is coming,"* or "No, he is not coming"?

"He did not say that he was not coming," repeated the young show official with a straight face.

That was the message from China—the house at this casino. *You are invited to play the game; you may enter and stay on our terms. If you choose to leave, then you bear the consequences.*

Eventually, around 9 P.M., the minister did arrive, surrounded by half a dozen smiling security personnel. He weaved his way briskly through the British pavilion and offered on-the-move handshakes, like the U.S. president working a crowd of admirers at a rally. Then he floated through to the next pavilion. The entire encounter at the British stand lasted less than forty-five seconds.

This was not the kind of environment that General Motors, the world's largest automaker, would easily adapt to, let alone find alluring. In fact, many inside GM in the early 1990s wanted no part of China. GM had problems enough at home. The company had lost a shocking $25 billion in 1991. There were deliberations at the board level about whether or not to declare bankruptcy—a fate that eventually did befall GM, eighteen years and tens of billions of dollars in losses later.

Business pressures were just one reason for General Motor's reluctance to enter China. An even greater inhibitor was the GM corporate culture that Steven Rattner, the automotive czar appointed by President Obama to oversee GM's 2009 bankruptcy, would later call "friendly arrogance." The people who ran the company had a penchant for feigning polite interest in the opinions of outsiders and then abruptly ending the discussion by saying "Oh, yeah, that's a good idea. We've already looked at that." GM knew better.

When a Detroit native visited Thailand 1993, he could not help but notice the sheer number of BMWs and Mercedes plying the streets of downtown Bangkok. GM had just opened a representative office in Thailand and placed a team there to develop new business. The Detroiter proposed the idea of marketing Cadillacs in Thailand to compete with the German luxury cars there. The response from GM's top guy in Thailand was friendly, but curt. "Yeah, thanks. You know, we already looked at that, and the time is just not right." End of discussion.

In China, GM found a country that was similarly unresponsive to the opinions of others. China knew that it wanted to build its own automotive industry. And officials in Beijing put in place the rules for any car maker interested in joining the effort:

1. No foreign company can produce cars in China without first forming a joint venture with a Chinese partner.

2. The foreign share of ownership may not exceed 50 percent.

3. To form an automotive joint venture, a foreign company must first secure approval from the central government. All models to be produced by the joint venture must also secure prior approval.

A list of discouragingly prohibitive rules was often followed by declarations that China enthusiastically welcomes investments by foreign companies. China genuinely wanted foreign companies to invest. But businesses would have to develop on China's terms and schedule. "Jump in, the water's fine," was the soothing, if misleading, message from the regulatory agencies.

GM eventually decided to do something, even if turned out to be the wrong thing. At the end of 1991, only four foreign companies—Volkswagen, Citroën, Chrysler, and Peugeot—had secured the right to produce their cars in partnership with Chinese companies. The basic strategy among foreign car companies was to break into the market and secure a foothold.

GM's first major testing of the waters came in 1992 when it formed a joint venture to build S-10 pickup trucks in the hard-scrabble northeastern city of Shenyang. The joint venture was given permission to build pickup trucks—but not sedans. The previous year, China had granted car-making licenses to First Automotive Works–Volkswagen, a joint venture between the Chinese central government and Volkswagen, and to Dongfeng-Citroën, a partnership that featured central government ownership alongside the French company. The door to new car licenses was shut tight, at least for the foreseeable future.

Although China looked likely to keep a tight lid on the car licenses for many years to come, trucks were different. China was prepared to offer a license to build GM trucks immediately.

The truck project in Shenyang appealed to GM management in North America for the simple reason that GM excelled in trucks, and its truck division was the company's only real moneymaker. GM trucks were good products, and the market had responded to that. GM also had faith that China, as a developing economy, would see explosive demand for pickup trucks in line with economic expansion. This had been exactly the case in Thailand, which is second only to the United States for pickup truck demand.

Pickups are the quintessential work vehicle at engineering and construction sites across America. Therefore the Chinese would naturally be drawn to trucks, too. That was the thinking at GM.

So much attention was focused on a strategic entry that GM probably looked closely at market demand only after the investment funds were committed. Had they done their due diligence, GM would have realized that Chevrolet pickups were going to appear on the Chinese market at the wrong time and in the wrong place. There were four primary contributing factors:

First off, the market structure was nothing like it was in the United States. Ninety-five percent of car demand was driven by government officials and state enterprise executives who were spending state funds. These people did not actually drive the cars—they were comfortable sitting in the back seat, being chauffeured around the city. Pickup trucks, in their eyes, were basic work vehicles designed for low-income farmers in the countryside. It would be far beneath their station to be seen in a pickup truck.

City dwellers in China carry a thinly disguised contempt for people who hail from the countryside. Shanghai denizens, exasperated with the slow wit of people from Beijing—or anywhere outside of Shanghai for that matter—often refer to non-Shanghainese as "*tu.*" "*Tu*" translates as "earthy" and carries the same connotation as "country bumpkin." Being driven around in a pickup truck would instantly place you in the category of *tu* and render you the laughingstock of your social circle.

Second, in the early 1990s very few farmers were even able to scrape together enough money to purchase a pickup truck. Instead, they bought tiny micro trucks and micro vans made by Chinese companies with technical assistance from Japanese brands Suzuki and Daihatsu. Those runabouts were usually priced at about $3,000. The Chevrolet S-10, starting at $18,000 was in a no-man's-land: far too rich for farmers and far too lowly for the image-conscious people in government.

Third, China's vehicle market was extremely parochial and region-centric. Government agencies and state enterprises in Shanghai bought cars built in Shanghai, at the strong behest of the Shanghai government. The same buy-local mandate was also true in the other car cities of Tianjin, Beijing, and Guangzhou. If you had visited Shanghai in the early 1990s, you would have seen a sea of Shanghai-built Volkswagen Santana sedans and only a tiny smattering of other car brands.

Last, a successful vehicle joint venture in China required a very supportive local partner located in a city where there was a decent level of income. Shenyang, a city of nine million in Northeast China, was the poster child for China's rustbelt, resembling hard luck cities like Gary, Indiana, or Pittsburgh, Pennsylvania, in the mid-1980s. Not exactly fertile ground for selling very expensive pickup trucks.

In the September 2008 *GM Next Update*, former GM chairman John F. Smith recalled GM's first steps in China:

> [GM's efforts in China] started long before 1998 and one of our first ventures was up in Shenyang. That was pretty rugged. Shenyang wasn't a main city [in China]. I remember Lou Hughes [president of GM International Operations from 1994–2000] saying, "if you go to Shenyang, it is not the end of the earth, but you can see it from there." There were no hotels, the GM people who went there were true pioneers. They sucked it up to get it done. That was never a very successful venture, but it was a start.

The absence of both a ready market and a proactive partner did not stop GM from forming a $132-million joint venture to build the American pickup trucks for the China market. Not long after the ink was dry, GM realized that the Shenyang project and several other smaller projects in China were forging ahead without any clear strategy. There was one deal to sell an engine line in Beijing and other deals to sell used equipment to other companies in China, but little else.

So GM had managed to plant its flag in China, but the hoped-for solid ground felt more like quicksand. Even as a new CEO, Smith understood that to get traction in the market, he needed people who knew China.

In February 1992, GM hired Richard Swando, a cagey China veteran. Swando, who had arrived in China in 1983, was one of the very first foreigners to work at Chrysler's Beijing Jeep joint venture. He was there when Chinese managers at Beijing Jeep insisted on keeping beds in the office for afternoon naps. He was there when the joint venture ran out of foreign exchange and operations nearly came to halt. He was there when the foreign executives at Beijing Jeep would gather at the Holiday Inn on Friday evenings for dinner, beers, and feisty exchanges until the early hours of Saturday morning.

"I was there from the beginning and saw a whole lot of things," he later said about his experiences at Beijing Jeep. He was about to see many, many more.

4

THE BACK DOOR

One of the things Rick Swando knew very well was that, if you managed to get things right, China's car business could be very lucrative. "We used to practice the sour face for the media. There was just no way we could let it be known just how much money we were making. It was a lot, and the Chinese government would not have been very happy if they knew just how much."

Educated at the University of Detroit, Swando was a pragmatist who quickly adjusted to China's rhythms. He hoped that one day GM could get into a joint venture with the city of Shanghai because "[the Shanghai people] were the only people in China who understood that to make a lot of money, you need to let your foreign partner make some money too."

Swando also knew that he needed to show results. He was the new guy on the block, a Chrysler guy. GM executives never had much respect for Chrysler guys. From GM's point of view, Detroit's auto industry consisted of GM (the perennial front-runner) and Ford (the occasional challenger). Chrysler was a mere also-ran, hardly worth talking about.

But Swando's opportunities for quick wins were limited. After the Chinese central government issued fresh car joint venture licenses to Volkswagen and Citroën in 1991, it had announced a moratorium on new joint venture production licenses. There was no timetable for when the door might reopen.

What the Chinese authorities did not mention in public was a gaping back door called Hong Kong. Clever traders in Hong Kong were connecting with authorities in southern China to skirt the rules set by Beijing and get imported cars into the country.

But GM was not set up to export cars, and the trading going on down in Hong Kong looked dirty, not the kind of activity that GM would stoop to. "The Japanese had trading companies to handle the messy stuff, and we never really considered going there," recalled one GM executive.

Without a license to make cars and without a backdoor play through Hong Kong, Swando faced the prospect of spinning his wheels for years. To just show up at the office and fax meek status reports home to Detroit like a bureaucrat was not an option. It wasn't Swando's way. He understood that he must work on something big, something with far more upside than the messy Shenyang truck deal. But what could he do?

He considered his competitors. Ford, Mercedes, Toyota, Honda, and Nissan still wanted to crack the market, too. They knew that the license door would reopen eventually. But the ministry officials in China gave no hint as to when or where. As a result, car companies bided their time by planting representative offices in Beijing and making regular visits to officials at the Ministry of Machine Building Industry, the gatekeepers of the car assembly licenses.

Swando made his own visits in Beijing, too. But his experience in China told him that the opening for a new car assembly license was more likely to spring up from below than to appear from on high. That was how change occurred in China—from below. It was true that the central government had sole authority to grant new car assembly licenses. But it was equally true that, in China, the impetus for a new license would likely originate with some unexpected event in some place far from the capital.

While Swando was making ritual trips to Beijing, he kept a sharp eye trained on what was happening at the provincial and city levels. There was one ongoing occurrence that gave him no end of frustration. Toyota, Honda, and Nissan did not have licenses to produce cars in China. But, since the mid-1980s, you would see imported Japanese cars all over the streets of China's richest cities: Beijing, Shanghai, and Guangzhou. This was akin to visiting a dry county in Kentucky and finding everyone out on their front porch swigging a cold beer. China was flatly against imports and erected a stiff 150-percent duty on cars from overseas. Yet the Japanese brands were everywhere you looked—taxi fleets, government officials cars, joint venture companies, you name it.

What the hell was going on?

In the early 1990s, Toyota, Nissan, Honda, and Mazda, along with their powerful trading companies, quietly operated giant offices in Hong Kong. Thousands of people employed by these companies were busy getting Japanese cars into China. The Japanese had discovered ways to export their Japan-built cars, via Hong Kong, to cash-paying customers inside mainland China. So many were the cars coming across the border, and so visible were they in China's main cities, that the only possible conclusion was that the authorities knew about it—and had a hand in the action.

The irony of the situation was not lost on Swando. On the one hand, officials in Beijing were proclaiming an ambition to build China's own automotive industry. At the same time, thousands of Japanese cars were leaking into the country every month. While Western companies obediently queued up in China for the right to invest and partner with the government for access to the car market, the Japanese were busy shipping their cars, at great profits, into the same market.

So which was it? Did China genuinely want to build an auto industry? Or did it want to present that face, while still condoning— even collaborating with—backdoor trade deals with the Japanese?

For officials in the central government, a strong car industry was the number one priority. But the provinces and cities could not have cared less about industry when there was an opportunity to make a quick buck through imports.

One channel was China's foreign joint venture company law. Tens of thousands of foreign joint ventures were being formed in China in the early 1990s as American, European, and Asian companies came searching for opportunities. Each of them, of course, required transportation.

Powerful officials in Beijing in charge of attracting overseas investors saw that the old cars on offer from China's licensed carmakers—Shanghai Volkswagen, Beijing Jeep Chrysler, and Guangzhou Peugeot—could kill investors' enthusiasm for doing business in China. They decided to waive the 150-percent duty on imported cars for this special class of buyers. Foreign joint ventures were permitted to import cars duty-free.

That policy triggered a frenzy of activity. Soon, hundreds of new Chinese "consulting companies" sprouted up in southern China near Hong Kong. Their business: formation of "paper" foreign joint venture companies. The process was simple. The consulting companies would identify a foreign company name and address already inside China, pair it with a Chinese firm's name, and then register a new company.

In most cases, these "overnight" foreign joint ventures never had any legitimate operations. But each one secured the paperwork allowing them to import one or two cars duty-free. For these consulting companies, registering a new foreign joint venture was like printing money. For the Japanese car companies, the fabricated joint ventures meant risk-free exports to China.

China's second channel for imports was the practice of *shui huo* or "water goods." There are scores of small tributaries that spread like slender fingers from the Pearl River into the South China Sea, around Hong Kong. Specially designed speedboats picked up new Japanese (and some German) cars from docks in Hong Kong and smuggled them under the cover of night to locations on the other side of the Chinese border. By skirting the 150-percent duty, these water goods traders earned huge profits moving Honda Accords, Toyota Crowns, Nissan Cedrics, and various Mercedes into China. The trade from water goods transport was so prolific that the process almost certainly involved participation from the customs department and the provincial police. Everyone got some money.

An auto industry supplier based in China recalled a reception in Beijing one evening in 1993: "The guy sitting next to me identified himself as a policeman and showed me his ID. When I asked him where he worked, he said: 'I smuggle cars down South. Pajeros are moving well right now.'"

Western car companies tended to think in terms of black and white. To them, success in China hinged exclusively on securing a car assembly license. But the Japanese took a more savvy approach, portraying respect for officials in Beijing while making money from exports through Hong Kong.

Twenty years later, in 2011, things have evolved, though these early interpretations of China and Chinese regulations remain relevant. And not just for the car industry. In sector after sector, from insurance to banking to retailing to apparel to the Internet, companies need a license to do most everything in China.

Google is only one of the most recent and visible examples of how China uses licenses as leverage. It also illustrates how Hong Kong still plays a role for companies trying to work around the rules. When the authorities in Beijing did not renew its license, Google rerouted its mainland customers to the Google Hong Kong home page. Chinese internet users could access the same Google services by simply using the backdoor that the Chinese language Google Hong Kong home page offered.

In 1992 and 1993, the levels of car imports—both legal and illegal—got out of hand. Larger sedans, imported mainly from Japan and Germany, nearly outnumbered the total number of cars built at the five approved foreign joint venture auto companies inside China.

Executives at Chrysler's Beijing Jeep joint venture were incensed by the car imports. Lauren Giglio, director of finance at the joint venture, appealed to his Chinese partners to help plug the import leaks. Their matter-of-fact response: "Those imports are not in our jurisdiction; they belong to the upper levels." Upper levels? That's the Chinese translation of their own *shangsi*—something like our term "higher-ups."

With China at that point importing tens of thousands of cars a year, hundreds of millions of dollars of foreign exchange were escaping the country. The flourishing trade in car imports eventually drew the attention of officials at the highest levels of power in the central government. They worried about the public's perception of government employees riding through the capital in the back-seats of Mercedes sedans, rather than in cars built in China.

In 1993, the central government ended the duty-free import provision for foreign joint ventures. Going forward, car buyers would have to purchase cars assembled in China, or cough up the staggering 150-percent import duty on the foreign-made car of their choice.

Terminating duty-free imports for foreign joint ventures should have been the end of the story for Japanese imports. But where there is money, tenacity of purpose is sure to follow. Not surprisingly,

Chinese traders and Japanese trading companies based in Hong Kong quickly devised new ways to deliver duty-free cars into the country.

A Chinese adage helps explain how events on the ground can continue to run counter to the mandates released from Beijing: *"Shang you zheng ce, xia you dui ce"* ("The top makes the policy, the bottom takes countermeasures"). Those are the words the team from Chrysler heard over and over again from traders and service shops when it made a special investigative trip to Guangdong Province. Chrysler had decided that if its partners in Beijing would not help, it would send a team to uncover what was going on. Three days into their visit, the team faxed back some startling findings:

- There are Toyotas and Nissans all over the roads here. Lots of Mitsubishi Pajeros, too. They are stealing our Cherokee customers.

- One Toyota service shop was huge. It was lunchtime, we had to wake a guy from his nap on the windowsill! He was wrapped in the curtain to keep warm so we didn't see him right away. He says business is "better than ever."

- Strangest thing. We're seeing Hondas and Nissans with funny Chinese character logos stuck on the trunks. Not sure what that's all about.

What that was all about was more trading innovation. Beijing's new policy insisted that cars be assembled in China, which should have meant more sales for the joint ventures. But the inventive people in southern China had other ideas. Within weeks of the release of the new policy, traders in Guangdong began to identify small state enterprises based there that, technically, possessed the rights to assemble vehicles.

These state-owned enterprises had names like the Fuhua Number 5 Assembly Factory or the Guangzhou Number 6 Tractor Works. Often consisting of not much more than an office and a small warehouse, these companies were vestiges of the 1960s when China attempted to spread industry as far and wide as possible. In the early 1990s, they might assemble five to ten 1960s-era buses or trucks a year. Many were completely idle.

The former importers of duty-free cars for foreign joint ventures now approached these "plants" with an offer to purchase the rights to their name. They also needed an okay to reproduce the factory's Chinese name in the form of a molded plastic logo. From there, the Chinese importers would place two orders with the Japanese trading companies in Hong Kong. One would be for a complete Honda Civic, minus the wheels and tires. The second order would be for the wheels and tires for that same Civic.

After receiving the separate shipments inside China (and avoiding the 150-percent duty on imported cars), traders would affix the wheels to the car (which was just enough to qualify the car as being locally assembled) and stick the rented tractor factory's plastic and chrome logo to the back of the car. Voila: one Chinese-produced car.

To observers from outside of China, it is hard to fathom that such wildly subversive practices would be allowed. Is China not a one-party system with extensive political and economic controls throughout the country?

Think of China as concentrations of power at the center and in the provinces. The ultimate power circle is the Chinese Communist Party, led by the Politburo in Beijing. But since Deng Xiaoping's reforms of the 1980s, China has become highly decentralized. Party officials at the provincial and city levels enjoy enormous leeway and power. When not tightly checked by the center, local officials can and do tend to work in cahoots with local business to create giant, profitable enterprises.

Luckily for Rick Swando, the people running the Shanghai power circle saw this national problem of runaway imports as an opportunity. The City of Shanghai soon declared that all government agencies and state enterprises owned by the municipality must buy cars built in Shanghai.

Next, Shanghai city officials began to conjure up grander ideas of how to fix the imported car problem once and for all—not just in Shanghai, but throughout the country. The best way to kill imports was to build good, modern cars inside China.

From the beginning, Swando had hoped for an opening with Shanghai. Now he was about to get one from an unexpected source: a talented young Chinese engineer named David Shi Chen.

The thirty-something Chen worked at the Robotics Lab in the GM technical center in Warren, Michigan. During a visit to his native China in the spring of 1992, Chen met China's Vice Premier Zhu Rongji, whom he had first gotten to know when Zhu led a senior Chinese delegation on a visit to GM in 1987.

Prior to the 1992 meeting with Zhu, Chen had been asked by Mr. Lu Jian, chairman of SAIC, to see whether Zhu would allow SAIC to set up a second car joint venture. Zhu told Chen, "If it is in Pudong, I don't see why not." Chairman Lu was happy to get this good news and shortly sent a formal letter to Chen inquiring about GM's interest in a joint venture.

Chen was a bit puzzled by the letter. "Why go through me, a junior engineer?"

Chairman Lu replied: "It is better to go through you first, unofficially. That way, if GM says no, there's nothing lost."

When he got back to Detroit, Chen met with Swando and gave him the news. To stop the flood of imports, the country needed to build a high-quality, modern, luxury sedan inside China. SAIC wanted to know: Was GM interested?

When Swando first got word of this from Chen, his gut told him that this was GM's big opening in China. Swando also knew that one of the first questions coming from his bosses would be: "Okay, that's good news, Swando. But tell us, has this Shanghai program gotten approval from the central government?"

If pressed, Swando could respond: "Well, the central government did not say that it did not approve the Shanghai program."

5

THE HOOK

"Right now, Ford is out front," was the word from SAIC officials to their prospective partners at General Motors.

This irresistible bait was dropped squarely into the rarefied air of the executive floor of GM world headquarters in Detroit. It was bait that GM's top executives would find impossible to ignore: Ford had a head start on GM to "win" the China luxury sedan program. For the leadership at GM, the mere idea of being beat by Ford anywhere at anytime was simply intolerable. That Ford might somehow outmaneuver GM in the world's most important growth market went beyond the pale. GM would be forced to act.

GM's view on competing with Ford is reminiscent of how Michael Lewis describes investment bankers' mentality in *The New, New Thing*: A handful of powerful New York investment banks had lent or invested tens of millions of dollars into a California start-up company with promising market potential. One year later, however, the start-up had not found the necessary customers. It was losing millions of dollars every month. With cash flow dangerously low, the company invited the investment banks for a fresh round of financing. But the banks, this time around, had changed their minds. Their united message, delivered in curt language, left no room for negotiation: "There is no justification for tossing more good money after bad." The bankers wanted out.

But then the founder of the start-up company rose from his chair and declared that he would use his (formidable) personal money to finance future growth. He'd buy out the bank loans and investments, too, since they had clearly lost confidence in the venture. The bankers' stomachs churned and collars felt tighter at this unexpected and uncomfortable news. Eventually, the bankers reversed their decision and joined in the new round of financing. For the bankers, the possibility that the company founder might turn out to be right about his company's future while they watched from the sidelines was infinitely more distasteful than the prospect of risking—and losing—tens of millions of more dollars of their own money.

Likewise, GM could not let Ford get out in front in China, no matter the consequences. With a few choice words, SAIC had created a race between the world's two largest car companies for the "right" to invest hundreds of millions of dollars in China.

SAIC's creation of a bidding war to invest cash and transfer technology turned convention on its head. In America, car companies routinely made states bid against one another for the opportunity to win new investments. The winner would get a fresh infusion of cash and technology, both of which would lead to new jobs and a higher tax base for the state.

In contrast, in China GM was about to queue up for the right to contribute gifts, much as tributaries had done for the emperor in Beijing for centuries. Keep in mind that in the mid-1990s China was not yet the export powerhouse it is today. Its car market was about the same size as Thailand's, and many, many companies from around the world had already been burned by the bitter experience of losing large amounts of money in the Middle Kingdom. Yet by merely noting that Ford was in the lead, SAIC had transformed its position from one of seeking investment to one of bestowing favors in the form of selecting a winner.

Rick Swando may or may not have completely appreciated SAIC's clever tactics at the time. Even if he did understand their cunning dimension, he might have hugged the SAIC officials anyway, just for creating some good news.

He needed good news. Swando's job was to get GM on track in China and the projects he inherited were in very poor shape. GM's two highest-profile initiatives in China—Brilliance GM and the BeiNei Engine plant—were embarrassments. At Shenyang Jinbei, operations were going from very poor to even worse. The original strategy in entering the joint venture was to produce the S-10 pickup truck. Before GM's arrival, the Jinbei operation used machines and processes that were decades old, leading one GM executive to tell a reporter from the *New York Times* that the plant featured "1920s technology."

When it hit the showroom, the S-10 carried a sticker price of $22,000, much higher than forecasted, and double the price of its nearest competitor. GM's spokesman in Hong Kong put on a brave face when asked about the poor performance, saying that "[GM] did not go to China only to pull out after a year or two."

Between the start of production in May 1992 and the end of 1993, the Shenyang Jinbei joint venture produced only five hundred S-10 pickup trucks—or just about three vehicles every other day. Worse yet, they had managed to sell fewer than thirty units! Even when the company managed to fob some trucks off on the rare customer, collecting payment became extraordinarily difficult. Customers would routinely declare themselves unable to pay and then advise Jinbei GM to collect money from other companies who owed them money. Sometimes payment from these third parties would come more than a year late. Or it might never come at all. Other times, the third parties offered goods from their own factories—textiles, shoes, furniture—in place of cash.

Swando and his spokesman both realized that if things did not improve fast, GM might just be forced to retreat. It was one thing to have a money-losing operation in Shenyang, China's rust belt, where unemployment rates were some of the highest in China. But now GM was striking out in another venture right inside the capital, under the gaze of both the city and the central government.

In the late 1980s, GM had aligned itself with the Beijing Number 1 Internal Combustion Engine plant—BeiNei ("BayNay") for short. BeiNei, like most engine plants in China in the 1980s, was producing motors with technology dating from the late 1950s and early 1960s. The central government funneled fresh money to these plants with orders to modernize, upgrade, and improve the quality of their products. *Engines are the heart of vehicles*, officials reasoned. *If we are to build a world-class auto industry, we must have our own modern engine plants.*

GM identified—and BeiNei management selected—an engine line from one of the Pontiac plants in Oklahoma. The line was disassembled, shipped across the Pacific, and installed in Beijing.

But both GM and BeiNei neglected one crucial variable: Who would buy the new engines? In the past, BeiNei had never had to consider this question. Under China's planned economy, BeiNei would be assigned a production target for the year. Then some other work unit or factory would get orders to purchase all of the manufactured engines from BeiNei. But under China's reforms, the guaranteed customers melted away. BeiNei needed to build *and sell* its own products, a concept that was completely novel to its management team.

GM made nice money—tens of millions of dollars—by selling the engine line to BeiNei. But the company looked bad to the more progressive and reform-minded officials in Beijing. "Mr. Swando, Mr. Swando, come on now, what is this?" officials would say with a look of deep disapproval. They knew that GM knew better than to sell engine line technology to an engine plant with no customers. Swando had inherited two losers, and he had to cope.

As a result, the BeiNei plant sat completely idle most of the time. "It was what we called 'engine line theatre,'" recalls one GM engineer involved in the project. "Any time there was a high-ranking government official in the neighborhood, we'd invite them over, turn on the lights, and crank up the line for a show. It looked pretty impressive." Once the visiting officials had completed their inspection, the workers and management team would return to playing cards or taking naps.

In the minds of the BeiNei management, they had achieved the central goal of getting modern engine technology. The market was an entirely separate matter, far from their reach or experience. "The sales volumes would never get above one thousand to two thousand engines a year because there were never any real customers," said the same GM veteran.

Swando also understood that GM's problems in China paled in comparison to the pressures in the home market. Without the "Ford factor" there would probably be no appetite for further investments in China.

Fortunately for Swando, in late 1992 GM had appointed a new leader named Jack Smith. His predecessor, Robert "Bob" Stempel, had been unceremoniously forced out. Outside board members—led by John Smale, the energetic former Chairman of Procter & Gamble—had orchestrated a classic boardroom coup. Smale became chairman, and Jack Smith assumed the title of president and CEO.

Smith had previously led GM Europe and had made money there. He understood the need for GM to pull its head out of the sands in Detroit: the company required more international operations. GM remained (barely) solvent at the time, thanks largely to profits from international operations in Europe and South America. In 1991, the company lost $7.1 billion on its North American operations but made almost $2 billion outside of the home market.

With Smith's drive for a more global presence came new appointments and more money. Smith named Louis Hughes as vice president of international operations in Geneva.

Many powerful people at GM headquarters remained very wary about China, given the nasty stings in Shenyang and the fiasco at BeiNei. But Smith ultimately approved a budget large enough for Swando to shift from his offshore perch in Hong Kong, the original headquarters of GM Asia Pacific, to a modest foothold in Shanghai in early 1995.

The money Smith was able to channel to China for this "special project" was a fraction of the investment made by Ford. GM China's original team consisted of just four people—Swando, Chen, and two Chinese staffers—who worked from the modest confines of two converted rooms at the Holiday Inn in Shanghai. Officials at SAIC were taken aback at the bare-bones GM presence in their city. The Chinese were not sure whether it was a sign that GM was not really serious about the luxury car program or if the tiny presence and locale was a sign of a new frugally minded GM under Jack Smith.

For Swando, the SAIC opportunity dwarfed anything he had seen before in China. In early discussions, SAIC officials hinted at a billion-dollar joint venture with initial capacity to build a hundred thousand cars a year. With this sort of opportunity beckoning, there was no reason for GM to continue messing around with chicken-shit programs like Shenyang Jinbei and BeiNei.

At Beijing Jeep, Swando had witnessed how even a modest car joint venture in China could make terrific profits. The key was to get inside China's protected industry and let the Chinese partners win production orders from the government. "We used to know our profits for the year by the first week of January, when we got the official production orders," recalled Kerry J. Ivan, a former director of finance at the joint venture.

American Motors' initial investment into Beijing Jeep was just $8 million. That cash infusion had secured a 37-percent share of the joint venture when it was formed in 1984. Within five years, the Beijing Jeep joint venture was quietly turning profits of $90 million annually. If GM could get together with SAIC on a luxury car program, the profits on $40,000 sedans would be through the roof.

But getting there would not be easy. Ford was already out in front, and the tough negotiators from SAIC would, no doubt, exact a mighty price from GM before awarding the project the world's number one automaker.

To get a sense of how negotiations go in China, one must make a visit back in time to the XiangYang market, an outdoor bazaar that covered an area of several city blocks on the fringes of the old French quarter in downtown Shanghai.

Prior to its closure by city officials in 2006, the XiangYang market sold every variety of brand-name consumer goods, from Armani jackets to PING putters to Gucci bags to Omega watches. All of these consumer products were for sale every day of the week, from vendors situated in row upon row of individual fifty-square-foot stalls. Out in front of the stalls, the vendors, portable calculators in hand, beckoned and coaxed shoppers with an enticing repertoire of offers:

"Rolex watches! Coach bags! Good quality! Special prices for you! Come looka!"

"TaylorMade, full set of clubs, plus tote bag, plus umbrella, so cheap! Deliver to your office or home!"

"Try on. North Face jackets! Very good price! Try it on, c'mon!"

All of the goods for sale in the XiangYang market had one thing in common: they were counterfeit. All of them were knockoffs—reasonable facsimiles of the much more expensive genuine articles. In most, the differences were subtle. But once in a while, one might see "VERSACE" engraved backward on buttons so that they read "ECASREV." OK, so maybe not all of the items were such reasonable copies.

Nevertheless, foreigners and Chinese alike flocked to the XiangYang market, drawn by the prospect of scoring an original-appearing item for just a fraction of the price of the real deal. A genuine Louis Vuitton bag at the authorized shop on Huaihai Road might cost $600. At XiangYang, a quality duplicate might go for $200 or $80 or maybe even as little as $60. The difference between what shoppers were willing to pay for a fake (an enticingly small fraction of the price of the genuine article) and what the trader had actually paid for the fake was where the traders made their money.

After all, what is the right price of a brand-name product that is, ultimately, just a copy of the original item? If the value of the brand is conceptual, then it follows that the price for the product would be conceptual too.

That is why the hustlers at the XiangYang market, as a rule, always began negotiations by asking the shopper what he or she was willing to pay. *Always.* That way, if the shopper guessed high from the beginning, then the seller would make a fat profit with almost no effort. If the shopper declined to open the bidding, then the vendor would start out with an extremely high price, nowhere near his final price target.

For shoppers just arriving from overseas, getting a $600 Louis Vuitton bag for $450 might look like a great deal. "Hey, I just got a 30-percent discount!" But for people who have lived and worked in Shanghai, it was understood that to pay anything more than $60 for the bag was to get ripped off.

There was nothing inauthentic about the Shanghai Auto Industry Corporation (SAIC) or its desire to build luxury cars for the domestic market. The company had built and run a profit-able joint venture with Volkswagen since 1985. But when SAIC first approached GM, the China national luxury car program was hardly more than a concept. It was an idea, like many generated in China, that might or might not lead somewhere. There were many reasons to believe that this particular concept of a luxury car program might never see the light of day.

For starters, not all central government planners were in favor of the program. They had already authorized production of the Audi 100 model at First Automotive Works–VW, a newly approved joint venture. The Audis would be more than adequate in size and stature to service the needs of government officials and state enterprise executives. SAIC found a way of fitting in with the rules set by the central government, while pursuing its own ulterior objectives. Said one GM executive involved in the early communications, "When SAIC first came to GM, they asked about building a minivan together. Only later they made clear [that] what they really wanted was a large sedan."

Volkswagen was against the program, too. It enjoyed a strong relationship with SAIC and cringed at the idea of GM or Ford or any competitor moving into "their" backyard of Shanghai. With its second joint venture in the north, Volkswagen accounted for 50 percent of cars produced in China, dominating the industry.

In 1993, there was no reason to believe that China could effectively stem the flow of illegally imported cars either. Even after the joint-venture duty-free import loophole was closed, Japanese and German cars continued to flow into the big cities. The "bottom's countermeasures" continued to outflank the "top's policies" in China.

What if GM invested hundreds of millions of dollars, built modern Buick sedans in Shanghai, but customers still opted for imported Japanese cars? A preference for Japanese cars over Buicks was already a reality in America, GM's home ground.

And yet, despite the cavalcade of reasonable doubts, the SAIC officials presented the program as a "go" and invited GM and Ford and Toyota to present their respective ideas for partnership. Like shopping at the XiangYang market, the best offer would determine the value of the theoretical project.

SAIC, of course, enjoyed one important edge over the traders in the XiangYang market. While XiangYang vendors had to compete with rival shops selling identical items (shoppers needed only to stroll a few yards to find the exact same items for sale), for Ford, GM, and Toyota, SAIC represented the only show in town.

That frightened both GM and Ford executives responsible for penetrating this important market. As an executive from Volvo explained at the time: "No executive with hopes for a career wants to be known as the one who lost China."

In retrospect, it is easy to see that the luxury car program was one well worth pursuing. But that was not at all evident in 1993. China was still a risky place to do business. The tactical negotiating excellence of the Shanghai officials had swung the balance decidedly in China's favor. There were two giant American car companies on the hook, chasing a singular opportunity in China.

And so the bidding began.

6

A REALITY SHOW

Companies investing in China must clear two key hurdles when forming joint ventures valued in the hundreds of millions of dollars. The first is to arrive at a basic agreement between two partners. The second is to conduct a feasibility study and work out the detailed business plan. In 1993, Swando and Chen entered their prolonged and tense Phase One. Much of their work involved showing products and technology in an effort to convince delegates from Shanghai that GM would be a better partner than Ford.

SAIC made fact-finding visits to Detroit that rapidly took on a likeness to the reality TV show *The Bachelor*, albeit ten years before that show's time. For the first few days of a visit to Detroit, the Chinese delegates from SAIC would spend all of their time with GM people in Detroit and at the GM tech center in Warren, on the east side of town. Then the Chinese would say a polite goodbye to GM and drive thirty-five minutes to the west side of town to Ford headquarters in Dearborn for the remainder of their trip.

SAIC's visits to Detroit were frequent enough to create a new term: "China vans." Ford, GM and Chrysler all lent vans to delegations visiting from China. It was the easiest way for the groups of six to eight people to get around town. You knew a China van by the scuff marks, the stained floor carpets, and the stale air from cigarette smoke. "We used to wonder if they weren't sleeping in the vans. The seats were beat up, scuff marks everywhere, and no matter what we did, we could not get the smell of smoke out," recalled one executive. "No one else [in the company] would touch the things."

No one ever mentioned the sorry state of the "China vans" to the Chinese. To complain about the dirty vans would be to risk early elimination from the contest. Instead, GM kept the vans in a special area and rolled them out only the next time a China delegation was coming through town.

For the Chinese, the vans were not their personal property. They belonged to someone else. And, as with the assets in the state enterprises where they worked, there was no incentive to keep them neat. (One still sees this in Chinese state companies today. A typical executive's office is large and neat and well-appointed. But the building's common areas are ragged and dirty from prolonged neglect.)

From time to time, the Chinese government posts large red and white banners that hang above city streets: "All of the power of the People's Republic of China belongs to the people." It is necessary to remind people that the state's power and property belong to them, the citizens of the P.R.C.

One thing the Chinese delegates from SAIC did not need reminding about was that they had GM and Ford exactly where they wanted them: in an epic race. Ford was quietly confident. Its prize horse was the all-new Mondeo sedan. Ford's brightest engineers worldwide had gathered together to create a "world car" ("Mondeo" originating from the Latin *mundus*), a car that appealed not only to customers in America but also to those in Europe and other markets.

Ford expected that the new Mondeo would be as much a winner as the Taurus had been during the 1980s. The Mondeo combined the spaciousness of an American sedan with the sporty looks of a European make. At the time of its launch, the Mondeo was called the "six billion dollar car." The effort was one of the most expensive new car development programs in the history of the industry. Ford's approach, trying to please all customers around the world with a single car, turned out to be a miscalculation. The Mondeo, with its mélange of features, never appealed strongly to customers in any one market.

The Chinese at SAIC were never enthusiastic about the Mondeo either. The central objection: Mondeo's sporty lines and unorthodox curves were too informal for government officials and state enterprise managers—the vast majority of car buyers in China. There was also some concern that the back seat did not offer quite enough room for passengers. But in the end their main objection was to the look of the car.

The China team at Ford listened carefully to the feedback and assured SAIC that it could make adjustments to the Mondeo to suit the Chinese market.

It will never be known whether SAIC could have learned, with time, to be content with Ford as its partner. But when you consider the Shanghai mindset, the strong preference from the beginning would have been to partner with General Motors. The City of Shanghai rates itself number one in the Middle Kingdom, several notches above other cities in China. It would be only fitting that Shanghai pair up with GM, the world's number one automaker. To form a joint venture with Ford might not have amounted to being *tu*, but it would certainly have been a step down.

Nevertheless, SAIC needed GM to table an offer at least as good as—and preferably a lot better than—Ford's. The Mondeo—aside from its "too-curvy" looks—was a very good car. SAIC needed GM to rally from behind in a hurry. Soon GM was complying with SAIC's wishes in a way that went well beyond Chinese expectations. Jack Smith was adamant that GM was to become a global company. China offered the perfect opportunity.

Smith's drive for change was urgent. GM's North American operations were a black hole: an albatross of legacy costs; an intransigent union; intense competition from the Japanese; a tumbling market share; and wounded brand reputations across several divisions, including Oldsmobile, Pontiac, Cadillac, and Buick. GM's international operations, on the other hand, offered some rays of hope. In Europe, South America, and Asia, GM enjoyed healthy growth and profits. Jack Smith clearly understood that to turn GM around, he needed to turn GM into a company that looked beyond Detroit.

GM's most powerful executives still ran the car divisions from Detroit. But there was a new tilt in the company in favor of overseas markets. For progressive international companies like Johnson & Johnson, such an adjustment would not seem out of the ordinary. But the move was groundbreaking for GM. Detroit was lost when it came to foreign markets. Younger GM executives heard rumors that GM's previous CEO, Bob Stempel, who was forced into retirement in late 1992, had never even set foot in Japan. (The rumor was untrue; Stempel was part of President George H.W. Bush's ill-fated "trade mission" to Japan in early 1992, where the president famously lost his lunch in the lap of the Japanese prime minister.) GM was just that parochial.

In *The Bachelor*, contestants can get knocked out after just one date. But SAIC was not in a hurry to eliminate Ford or GM. In the early meetings, Chairman Lu had told Swando to "get ready for a Long March," referring to the storied several-thousand-mile journey of the Red Army in the mid-1930s. Lu also told Swando and his team that Ford was proposing the Mondeo. What was GM's response going to be? GM's first proposal recommended that the joint venture produce something from the Chevrolet family. It was a new GM policy that Chevy would be the lead brand for all international markets.

SAIC felt lukewarm about Chevrolet. For starters, they rightly associated the name with the failing pickup truck venture up in Shenyang. Second, in their view the Chevrolet brand was too plain for their purposes. The intention, after all, was to build an impressive full-size sedan to displace the imports from Japan.

Swando then suggested Cadillac. No, SAIC said, Cadillac is too ostentatious, too over the top. The central government would kill the project if they were to see Cadillac on the cover page. Growing a little impatient, the SAIC team finally came out and named their target. What we really want, SAIC revealed, is Buick.

Buick? *Buick?* Swando's team was at a loss for words. Buick was the choice of the older set in America, the country club types who spent leisurely half days during the week playing golf and saving for their retirement homes in Florida. The average age of a Buick buyer was sixty. What would the Chinese want with an old folks' car?

The Chinese reminded GM that Buick had a history in China dating back to the 1920s. The last emperor's car was a Buick. In its heyday in the 1920s, Shanghai was a thriving center of international commerce, with thousands of residents from Europe and America. Buick was the king of the road in Shanghai in that era. The team at SAIC wanted to tap into the feel-good history.

As luck would have it, GM was working on a brand new Buick Century. Swando could not wait to show top-secret early versions of the car to Lu Jian and his team at SAIC. The new Century was spacious, had an imposing road presence, and offered more than ample power, delivered by its 3.1 liter V6 engine. Their eyes "got really big," said Swando, when they realized that this brand-new car could soon be built in Shanghai.

Later in the meeting room, the team from SAIC flipped through pages of their notebooks and pointed out two short-comings with the Century. The first was space. The Mondeo offered better overall room in the back seat. This was a crucial point, because most users of the car would be backseat riders, not drivers. What was the point of a large sedan if the back seat was cramped? And second, the Buick engine size at 3.1 liters was too large. To qualify for the project, the engine had to displace less than 3 liters.

Swando asked Detroit for urgent adjustments to the Century length and engine size. The North American engineers at Buick grudgingly complied but felt genuinely irritated by such requests. "You mean we have to invest in engineering changes to a product that may, in fact, never be produced in China?" they asked. "What if we lose to Ford—then who will pay for the engineering?" It was almost comical to witness how different priorities in the same company could create such tensions. "There was zero team-work," is how one participant summed up the situation. Others in Detroit voiced even greater skepticism: "Do they even have cars over there in China?"

For SAIC, the car—whether the Mondeo or the Century—was just one part of the deal. The Chinese also wanted assurance that the winner would be building plants in Shanghai to make key car parts. Jack Smith quickly sent a note to David Chen, who was still working in the robotics department in Warren: "Congratulations, David, you're going to lead ACG in China." ACG (Automotive Components Group) was GM's massive parts division, later named Delphi. Chen came home and told his wife he'd gotten an offer he could not refuse.

Chen worked side by side with Swando on the deal. His focus was to bring ACG engine, transmission, axle, steering, and braking systems to China. Ford wasted no time in promising SAIC that it, too, would bring key component investments to China.

In the twenty months from the middle of 1993 until March 1995, when the deal was finally awarded, GM and Ford each went through cycle after cycle of revised proposals in an all-out effort to deal a final death blow to their rival. SAIC representatives would always pull out their notebooks and mention something that the other company had offered, further fanning the flames.

The bids escalated, week after week. Only a few years earlier, Volkswagen had set the industry peak by investing $150 million in a joint venture with First Auto Works. Most of the value of Volkswagen's contribution came in the form of a used VW Jetta production line that was dismantled in Westmoreland, Pennsylvania, and shipped across the Pacific to China. Thanks to the escalating Ford and GM bids, the Shanghai deal was on track to reach $1 billion.

The pressure on people at Ford and GM was tremendous. It evoked the closing moments of an episode of *The Bachelor*: when the camera moves from the bachelor to each of the contestants and back to the bachelor again, it seems inevitable that one of the contestants will lose self-control and yell out: "You pick me, right?"

Ford could wait no longer. In late 1994, news was leaked to the media that Ford had achieved victory in Shanghai. But that announcement was premature and, much to Ford's embarrassment, false. Ford's misstep reveals one of the most basic business landmines in China. A deal of this magnitude—no matter how visible, no matter what the time deadlines, no matter what the spoken agreements—is never complete until it is signed and chopped by the highest authorities in the government.

The team negotiating the deal may never set eyes on the people who give the final approval and sign off. Those mysterious deciders are like a modern-day Wizard of Oz. You can have verbal agreements and even written agreements signed by people at the working level. And even the next level up. You can get a signed and chopped purchase order on official company stationery. But no agreement is valid until it is matched by a final signed and officially chopped agreement. No official chop? No deal. Nine of the ten required decision makers signed and chopped? No deal. Firm gentlemen's handshakes and earnest promises? Not a chance.

Even though Ford's media leak did not match the reality on the ground, the GM leadership in Detroit was stunned. Within hours of the news breaking over the wires, the GM office in Shanghai was bombarded with panicked calls from headquarters: "What on earth have you done to lose the bid?"

GM felt that it needed to act quickly and decisively. GM had come to understand that what mattered most to officials at SAIC was learning how to make cars on their own. Leading China's drive to build a car to call its own was, in fact, SAIC's original mission. The China strategy was as simple as it was straightforward:

Step 1. Form joint ventures with leading global carmakers.

Step 2. Absorb the foreign partners' technologies related to car design, engineering, and manufacturing.

Step 3. Build cars under China's own brand names.

For SAIC, the trouble was an inability to move beyond Step 1. Ten years after formation of the Shanghai-VW joint venture, the German automaker still held all of the keys to the kingdom of car making. Volkswagen was still totally in control of the design, engineering, and manufacture of the old Santana. SAIC managers took charge of distribution, handled the regulatory side of the business and, of course, worked side by side with VW on finances. But when it came to the art of building cars, the Germans operated alone. The fiercely proud city of Shanghai could not put together even such a basic model. This failure to capture the know-how of car making was a point of embarrassment and anxiety for SAIC.

Jack Smith decided that to win SAIC's hearts and minds, GM should invite Lu Jian, the chairman of SAIC, to view GM's Brazil operations, GM do Brasil, first-hand. This trip to Brazil, led personally by Jack Smith, would swing the bid once and for all in GM's favor. Over a period of three days, the Chinese would be escorted through every facet of GM do Brasil's operations: the engine plant, the paint shop, the transmission factory.

The trip proceeded, and at each plant, the Chinese executives listened to presentations given by GM's Brazilian managers. After each talk, the Chinese approached the presenter and asked his nationality.

"Well, I am Brazilian, of course," was the inevitable answer.

"You're not American?" asked the skeptical Chinese.

"No, I am pure Brazil."

The Chinese were astonished and energized. In GM do Brasil, they saw a blueprint for their own aspirations. One day China, too, could manage an operation like GM do Brasil on its own.

At the closing dinner of their visit to Brazil, Lu Jian stood up and offered some impromptu comments. Lu said that he was initially very skeptical about coming to Brazil. *Why would GM take us half way around the world?* But now they had seen the operations. Lu could "see the possibilities for our own future" in China.

The message to SAIC was clear: GM promised to approach the partnership in Shanghai the same way it did the Brazil business— by jumping in with both feet. GM would treat its 50–50 joint venture in China as if it were a 100-percent subsidiary. As evidence of its commitment, GM agreed to establish an R&D center in the Pudong area of Shanghai where the SAIC and GM would jointly develop and refine future products for the China market.

When Lu returned from Brazil, the Chinese media were naturally curious about his impressions. What is the status of the national large car program, and which bidder is in the lead? Lu deflected the direct questions and indicated that the race remained very tight, with GM and Ford both offering excellent business proposals.

One member of the media then asked about Toyota: were they still in the hunt?

"Toyota?" Lu replied. "Toyota's at the back of the line."

Indeed, this was a race between two rivals from Detroit. Toyota continued to ship tens of thousands of cars into China via Hong Kong and was never seriously interested in the bid. Even so, Lu could not resist the opportunity to set the Japanese automaker in its place.

In March 1995, SAIC informed GM that it had submitted the best overall bid and would be selected as SAIC's partner. But first, "final approval must come" from Beijing. That decision would not come until six months later. In October 1995, the *New York*

Times published an article about rumors that GM had won the bidding contest:

> Zhu Bingcheng, chief of Shanghai's automotive department, declined to confirm the decision, but did not deny it. "I can't answer the question on whether this corporation has decided to offer a big cooperative project to General Motors," Zhu said. Officials of Shanghai Automotive originally promised a decision on the joint venture by October 1994. Then they said February, then May, then by the end of the year. When GM's Chairman, John F. Smith, visited Shanghai last month, he laughed when asked when the announcement would come. "We really don't know," Mr. Smith said.

In November 1995, Beijing finally gave permission. SAIC and GM would invest $700 million in a green field flex plant to manufacture both the Buick Century and the Buick GL8 business minivan. The companies knew that there was an opportunity for their new product to displace hundreds of thousands of imports, which could generate head-spinning revenues and profits.

Rick Swando and his colleagues savored the moment. The initial goal had been accomplished. GM had beaten Ford. Again. It was the kind of black-and-white, winner-take-all, loser-go-home scenario that the competitive-minded Americans at GM could identify with.

But China is seldom, if ever, black and white.

PART TWO

POLE POSITION, YELLOW FLAGS

7

THE KIT PRICE

So, at long last, GM had emerged victorious over Ford. The battle, however, was ultimately about how much money and technology the American companies would bring to China. For SAIC, it was all upside.

Negotiations got much tougher in China when the issue was how the money should be divided. While GM was savoring its fresh engagement with SAIC, Beijing Jeep—the joint venture between the City of Beijing and Chrysler—was moving into its tenth year of marriage.

In the early years at Beijing Jeep, only two board meetings mattered. One was for planning. China's central government gave the Chinese-American joint venture an annual production target. A typical planning directive might read: "The State Planning Commission approves that Beijing Jeep produce 35,000 Jeep 212s and 8,000 Cherokees." The planning order was straightforward, black and white, like original orders in the army.

The other meeting was the one that Peter Badore, the ultra-competitive vice-president at Chrysler, enjoyed. He embraced the high stakes and the tension. It was at this meeting in 1992 that Badore and his Americans battled Chairman Wu and his Chinese contingent for the final say about the most important item on the agenda: the "kit price."

"Kit" is a car industry abbreviation for "knock-down kit," a collection of car parts packed into wooden crates and shipped from a factory in America to China for assembly. During the 1980s, China could make little beyond a few simple parts like tires, wheel covers, and windshield wipers. Thus Beijing Jeep was forced to import almost all the original parts from Jeep plants in America. The kits consisted of all kinds of car parts, including engines, transmissions, windshields, axles, brake parts, and even doors.

The "kit" in kit price refers to the large crate of imported automotive parts. "Price" refers to how much the joint venture, Beijing Jeep, would pay for the parts. The final kit price was critical to the bottom line. "The kit price was everything," said Kerry J. Ivan, former director of finance at Beijing Jeep.

Both the Chinese and the Americans pored over the math. If, for example, the price of a Cherokee sold in China was $35,000 and the gross margin was 10 percent, then the joint venture would earn $3,500 per vehicle. The American and Chinese partners in Beijing Jeep would divide that profit based on their equity shares. In this case, the City of Beijing owned 59 percent of the shares in Beijing Jeep and took a corresponding share of the profits. That formula was transparent to everyone. But the forty-five-year-old Badore and his Americans had another set of information that the Chinese could not access. He knew the cost of the parts in the kit. And he knew the profit margin. Chrysler, the parent company in America, made a handsome profit on every kit it shipped to China.

The Chinese management were obviously aware that Chrysler was making profits on the kits. But they did not know how much. What they did know was that the price to the consumer in China was fixed by the government. The joint venture had no authority to set prices. Therefore, the partners in the joint venture were forced into an awkward position of having to negotiate against each other for profits.

The higher the kit price, the more profits would flow directly to Chrysler in America. The lower the kit price, the more profit the Beijing Jeep joint venture would make. China owned a majority share in the joint venture, so naturally the Chinese executives at Beijing Jeep always tried to drive the kit price down.

Peter Badore was a wiry Vietnam War veteran with a wickedly high IQ and a passion for making a deal. He savored negotiating the kit price with his Chinese partners-cum-adversaries at Beijing Jeep. His Chinese counterparts, on the other had, could not stand his methods. Badore knew that the Chinese negotiators liked to make kit price talks long and irritating. The longer and the more irritating, the better.

After the thirteen-hour trans-Pacific flight, executives from Chrysler would typically arrive in Beijing feeling jet-lagged and short-tempered. The twelve-hour time difference disoriented even the most seasoned travelers. The longer the talks went on, the more likely it was that Chrysler would grant concessions. So had been the Chinese experience with American executives.

But Badore took a different approach that caught the Chinese off guard. He arrived in Beijing two days before the meetings were to begin, checked into a hotel room, and slept for the better part of forty-eight hours. Then, fresh and alert, he set out for the meeting.

There were thirteen board members: eight from BAIC and five from Chrysler, reflecting their 59/41 percent ownership split. Badore was chairman of the kit price board meeting. When he got inside the room, he announced two rules of engagement:

1. No sleeping is allowed.

For emphasis, Badore took a small stack of fresh five-dollar bills from his pocket, removed the top one, and slapped his Lincoln-laden hand hard against the wooden table. "Anyone who falls asleep will get a five-dollar fine."

The second rule?

2. No one leaves the meeting until a kit price is set.

The Chinese initially were not alarmed. Surely the Americans would fall asleep first. And they would also be the first ones wanting to get the meeting over with. But then Badore began to talk.

He talked about lots of things in addition to the kit price. He talked for fifty minutes about the superiority of American fighter jets. Then he described the latest American missile technology, with a detailed breakdown of the relationship between rocket fuel density and liftoff power. Then he talked about the pennant race and how many games the Detroit Tigers would have to win to clinch the division. His Chinese interpreter obediently translated his voluminous lectures to the best of her ability.

Initially, the loquacious Badore intrigued the Chinese board members. But after three hours of his monologue, they grew bored and restless. In other meetings, the Chinese board members would have started smoking to ease the tedium. But Badore was fanatic about prohibiting smoking during the meeting, so lighting up was out of the question.

Eventually, a Chinese director in the corner made the mistake of dozing off.

Badore shot up from his seat like a cobra—he'd been waiting for this moment. He extended his lean body across the table and slammed a fresh bill on the table in front of the sleeper.

Thwack! "That's a five-dollar fine!" he proclaimed with a look of reproach.

Then Badore resumed talking. And talking. And talking some more. Three hours became eight. The eight hours stretched into sixteen. Badore talked for sixteen hours without interruption, aside from a rare trip to the bathroom.

His nonstop discourse on all manner of topics had a specific purpose: Badore was determined to see Chrysler's position of the kit price prevail. For Badore, the price of the kit would be $13,000 each. For the Chinese, the price would be no more than $10,000. There was a gap of $3,000 per kit. That added up to millions of dollars, because the joint venture planned to build twenty thousand Jeep Cherokees in the coming year. If Badore got his way, it meant millions more dollars for Chrysler—and millions less for the Chinese.

There seemed to be no closing of the gap. So Badore kept talking through the evening and into the early morning hours. At daybreak, he was still holding court.

Throughout the night, Badore bolted out of his chair several times and slammed a $5 bill in front of snoozing board members. Each time he'd announce with some gusto, "No sleeping—that's a $5 fine!"

At the twenty-third hour, the senior Chinese executive, Mr. Wu, shouted in exasperation: "Okay, that's enough. We cannot go on like this forever. People have families to go home to, you know?" Wu wore the conservative communist party gray button-down tunic—the kind you see the leader of North Korea appear in today.

"All right, Mr. Wu," said Badore. "Let's have an agreement, you and me. I am going to flip this coin. And you call it. If you call it right, we will go with your kit price. But if you call it wrong, then my price stands."

"What?"

"We'll decide the kit price by flipping the coin."

"What? That is a crazy thing to say! This is a professional company, our joint venture. We have to act responsibly. A flip of the coin is no way to settle the kit price!"

The interpreter converted the Mandarin sloppily into English, but Badore could already measure the response from the body language. Chairman Wu's nostrils widened as he waved his arms in protest. The other Chinese looked stunned. The American lieutenants to Badore stared down at their notebooks and into their teacups. But not Badore. He was poker-faced as he fixed his eyes on his opposite across the boardroom table.

Wu continued, "There is nothing to talk about. A flip of a coin? That is a joke!"

"Okay, that's fine with me," Badore answered. "If we cannot flip the coin, then we'll just have to keep talking—and negotiating."

After thirty-six hours, Madam Wang, president of Beijing Jeep, interrupted Badore: "Okay, all right, that's enough! This time, and this time only, we go with your kit price! Can we all just go home now?"

Badore glanced at his watch and said, "Sure, now that we have an agreement on the kit price, it's time to go home. We cannot forget that some people owe the sleeping fines, though. Let's make sure the fines are included in the meeting minutes."

It was a bitter end to a long, long day. Wu and everyone else in the room understood that Chrysler enjoyed all the leverage. If Badore was ready for a coin flip, it meant that he had already won the negotiation, whatever the kit price.

Chrysler in America would surely take fat profits on the kits shipped to the joint venture. Then Chrysler would take 41 percent of the profits made by the joint venture. The Americans were making money twice on every Jeep built and sold in China.

When the participants rose from their seats to mark the end of the meeting, the Chinese bodies stood rigid with tension, their fists curled into tight balls, while the Americans quietly hustled out the boardroom doors.

Badore's decision to get tough with the Chinese did not come out of nowhere. For years, distrust had been building between Chrysler and the City of Beijing.

Just months earlier, the Chinese and Americans had agreed to increase Chrysler's equity in the joint venture in exchange for Chrysler's bringing over a set of stamping machines from Detroit. But, in an attempt to prevent Chrysler from capturing higher dividend payments that came with the higher equity share, the Chinese slow-walked their recognition of the increase.

Under the agreement, Chrysler would contribute eight presses to the Beijing Jeep joint venture. In return, Chrysler's equity share in the joint venture would increase from 38 to 41 percent. The lift in equity share had become quite valuable to Chrysler. Each year the now-profitable joint venture issued dividend payments to shareholders in the millions of dollars. Each percent increase in equity could mean $500,000 in additional annual dividends.

And as the joint venture got larger, the dividend payments would increase too. Even better, the dividends were paid back to Detroit in U.S. dollars. Every additional dividend dollar going into the hands of Chrysler meant, of course, one less dollar for the Chinese. Clearly, it was in the interest of the Chinese to delay the increase in Chrysler equity. But how?

Only weeks after the agreement was signed, the Chinese began to give a specific interpretation to the terms. Yes, the Chrysler equity in BJC should increase. But that share increase should become effective only after the presses were installed and working in the BJC plant.

In negotiations, a favorite tactic among the Chinese is to say the same thing over and over in slightly different ways. Sometimes they get a little emotional, raising their voices to express indignation or impatience. And they sustain their show of peevishness until the other side throws up its hands and says, "Okay, enough!"

The Chinese asked rhetorical questions by fax, by phone, and in person:

- How can the shares increase with the presses sitting in Detroit?
- What if the transport ship meets bad weather and sinks and the presses never arrive in China?
- Maybe there is something about the presses that we do not know. Why does Chrysler want to sell them to us?

The Chinese argued that they would not know if the machines were in good shape until they were on the ground in China. Worn-down Chrysler executives reluctantly agreed to the Chinese interpretation of the terms. But they soon began to feel regrets.

Chrysler's anxiety grew further when the Chinese announced that they would lease a Chinese ship and order it to Detroit to pick up the presses. There were plenty of ships traversing the Pacific, shunting goods between the United States and China. Why did Beijing Jeep insist on leasing its own ship for the job?

Chrysler was not about to allow the Chinese from BJC into their stamping plants, for fear that the Chinese would try to steal the technology. So, with the Chinese crew docked at the port in Detroit, poor communications slowed the effort to get the presses out of the Chrysler stamping plant where they were housed and onto the ship that was manned, naturally, by a Chinese-speaking crew. But this delay was just a short time-out compared to what was to come next.

Back in Beijing, the Chinese executives at BJC had decided to hire several dozen day-laborers from rural areas near the city, along with their sets of digging tools. Once the presses arrived in China, the workers began digging giant holes in the ground to create foundations. For the BJC plant manager, an American from the south, the scene was ludicrous. "Who are these guys digging up dirt with shovels when a machine could get the job done so much faster?" he demanded to know.

"Machines are too expensive," the leader of the Chinese crew explained. "If we use machines, the cost will be almost 600,000 RMB. But with our own hands, it is just 300,000 RMB." (In 1949, the communists renamed the *yuan*, the traditional Chinese currency, as *renminbi*, or "the people's [*renmin*] money [*bi*]"; RMB is the equivalent of our dollar sign. The people still use *yuan* as well as RMB and the informal *kuai*.)

The American plant manager knew from experience that, with the use of machines, the entire job should take less than two months. He asked the crew leader: "So, how long is this going to take your crew?" Arms crossed, he waited for a response.

Without blinking, the crew leader replied, "Eight months."

At this point, everyone at Chrysler realized what was really going on. "They wanted to go as slow as possible with the presses—just don't let Chrysler increase its equity and collect more dividends," recalled Lauren Giglio, director of finance at the joint venture between 1990 and 1993. "It was really ironic, because BJC could not expand and start making more money until the presses were in place. But the goal of delaying more dividends to Chrysler became more important than increasing the money for everyone."

Eventually, after eight months, the Chinese work crew got the digging done. The craters they had shoveled were very deep and very wide; workers climbed in and out of the eight holes like an army of ants. Getting the base of the stamping machine right is vital to its durability and accuracy. That takes time, particularly when done by hand. Four of the presses were put to work right away; the other four presses were in standby mode, waiting to go into action when the expected increase in demand for Cherokees kicked in.

Guo Weiming, deputy head of finance at BJC and Giglio's Chinese counterpart, finally made a special presentation to the BJC board of directors. In it he declared that because not all of the presses were operational, it would not be possible to increase Chrysler's equity or dividend payments. All the presses must be operational first.

Giglio recalled similar protests he had heard from his Chinese counterparts:

- Let's go over to the plant right now and see whether all the presses are in operation. If they are all in operation, then there is nothing to talk about. But we are here talking because the presses are not all working right now.

- Now is not the right time to increase Chrysler's equity and pay higher dividends. Besides, we did not even ask how much profit Chrysler is making sending us old presses.

- Don't you know we could have purchased the presses somewhere else?

If the Chinese recognized the equity increase too early, the joint venture would have to pay Chrysler more dividends—and payments would be made with precious foreign exchange ("forex"—U.S. dollars or any hard currency freely exchanged in international markets). "The Chinese never wanted to spend a penny of foreign exchange. For them, spending forex was like giving up your mother," said Giglio.

The Chinese stalling on the stampings obviously angered Chrysler. The ill will and money tricks at Beijing Jeep had been captured in an internal Chrysler memo three years earlier, in the weeks that followed the Tiananmen Square protests and bloody crackdown.

Memo to the Board of Management, Chrysler Corp.
Re: Where to From Here
Date: 22 June 1989

Stating the obvious, the insidious events on the morning of June 4 have had a sobering effect on all. Unfortunately, CMC [Chrysler Motor Corp.] cannot hope to have a meaningful partnership with a country headed by hard-line communist conservatives.

Because Beijing Jeep forms an intricate part of their bureaucratic system and at the corporate level we confess "old friends status" this is not and cannot be the case under the current system; e.g., today's Chinese directors have been and always will be cautious of Sino-American management integration into the running of BJC. This regime is likely to be with us for a long time.

Chinese strategy over the medium to long term is to absorb as much technology for their domestic requirements as possible. We are the price they must pay for this technology.

Recent bureaucratic bungling in the area of sales, pricing, distribution and FX [foreign exchange] availability coupled with ambiguous

(*Continued*)

customs and localization requirements [is] taking its toll on BJC. Sales are down, inventory up, capital expenditures continue at a rate unsupported by volume increases, money is hard to borrow and export demands by government remain unrealistic.

BAW's receivables have shot up to 30M [RMB]. CMC's ability to curtail this landslide, even when the events are anticipated, or to run BJC as a commercial venture, is very limited.

Assuming a re-entry, maximize profits and minimize risk for the remainder of the partnership term. "We're in the CKD business." [CKD is short for the "completely-knocked down" kit or the process of shipping boxes of car parts to China from America.]

1. Assist wherever possible in the day-to-day operations, e.g., fiscal responsibility. Management responsibility in an advisory capacity.

2. Let them spend whatever they want on the capital expenditures; recommend, but don't fight. It's the government's money anyway.

3. Stick hard and fast to CMC's quality standards. China does not have the infrastructure to make quality parts. The CKD business is with us for a long time.

4. Absolutely insist on BJC abiding by an open credit account policy.

5. Dividends. Our policy is realistic, politically we will have to re-invest 50 percent, but the remaining 50 percent we want each year.

The key recommendation in the memo was that Chrysler focus on staying "in the CKD business." That meant that the strategy of the American company was to manufacture parts at Chrysler plants in the United States and sell those parts (for a nice profit) to the Beijing Jeep Corporation, its joint venture in China.

If Beijing Jeep, in turn, made profits on the sale of the assembled Jeep in China, Chrysler would earn a second stream of revenues and profits. But the "source-plant" profits—profits made by sourcing parts from plants in America—were the priority. It was simple, from Chrysler's point of view: Why invest in manufacturing inside

China when you could still manufacture in Detroit and take profits by exporting parts to the joint venture?

The memo writer concluded with a candid assessment of the situation and a recommendation:

> The government, I believe, will eventually bail BJC out of trouble. However, the lesson for CMC is very clear: You cannot seriously consider BJC as a commercial venture that you can mold and use as a part of a global strategy if you have little or no control in its destiny and little faith in the government in which it operates.
>
> However, if you can supply it, we have them on the hook. And here is where CMC's strategy must lie—in the CKD kits.

To beat Ford, GM had promised SAIC a different kind of relationship—one of transparency, trust, and sharing. But how would the new partners tackle the tough and unavoidable issue of kits and kit prices—which is really a question of who gets how much money?

8

PUTTING SHANGHAI FIRST

Rick Swando had firsthand knowledge about the difficulties at Beijing Jeep. But he felt optimistic about SAIC because the Shanghainese understood that the foreigners "needed to make some money too."

In less than three years, Swando had achieved a small miracle, taking GM from the forsaken wilderness of Shenyang pickup trucks to the largest automotive deal ever completed in China. Now it was time to hand the baton over to Philip Murtaugh, the guy who would put the strategies and plans into action.

Murtaugh had moved into his position as general manager of GM's Shanghai Operations on January 1, 1996. At that point, the signing of the final joint venture agreements for Shanghai General Motors was still fifteen months away. He spent most of 1996 working out the details of the cooperation during long hours across a conference room table from SAIC officials.

Without some changes in GM's approach, however, this joint venture was in danger of turning out just like most of the company's other overseas partnerships: a dud. In the early 1990s Murtaugh had worked at Isuzu in Japan, where he learned to speak Japanese. More recently he had worked in Luton, England, where GM and Isuzu ran a failing joint venture. That company was a perennial money-loser, to the great frustration of General Motors.

Joint ventures anywhere are precarious. Both sides need to reach a clear understanding about each other's objectives and about where responsibility lies in the myriad factors that affect the business. Who's in charge of product planning? What will the dividend policy be? Most times, the objectives of the shareholders are partly aligned, at best. Over time, friction and tensions build as the two sides look out for their own interests. The Chinese have an expression for it: *Tong chuan yi meng*: "Sleeping in the same bed, dreaming different dreams."

Joint venture enterprises with imperfect alignment of interests inevitably suffer. Automotive joint ventures in China are particularly tenuous. The partners' main objectives are in complete conflict. Both sides want to make money—for themselves. One side has the technology and the other side wants to get its hands on it. Beijing Jeep was the perfect example.

Christmas Day in China is a day like any other ordinary day of the year. City people commute to office jobs and put in a full day of work without distractions. There are no Christmas cookies or punch in the office kitchen. No employee stockings to stuff or chocolates to share. There's no taking off early. It's just a regular day at work.

Consider the background: for Westerners, working on Christmas Day in China can amplify feelings of being far from home. To address this, most Western companies in China have Christmas parties where employees can gather to eat and drink and deepen bonds with their fellow foreign and Chinese workers. These holiday gatherings can also lead to strong feelings of friendship and loyalty among people who might otherwise remain strangers—something like what happens between soldiers in a foxhole.

Under Murtaugh, GM began its tradition of year-end Christmas parties in China in 1996. Though the formal joint venture contract with SAIC wouldn't be signed for another four months, GM felt that victory was near. And so, in the wet, gray days of December, when Shanghai is bone-chillingly cold but snow rarely falls, GM had its first Christmas gathering.

The event was held at the Yangtze New World Hotel. About two hundred people gathered for dinner and drinks, continuing on well past midnight. There were no memorable speeches or embarrassing cultural gaffes to talk about. But there was one remarkable thing about the party: the incredible variety of passports.

"We had twenty-two nationalities in attendance," said Murtaugh. "In addition to the Chinese and Americans, there were a lot of Germans, some Brazilians, and even some Argentinians."

What were people from twenty-two different countries doing at a General Motors Christmas Party in Shanghai? They were all employees of GM, each with his or her hands on some aspect of GM's fledgling enterprise in China.

GM was invading China in a particularly GM way. Top executives from GM's far-flung empire that spanned the globe wanted to make certain that they had people on the ground as part of the effort to "open up" China. That's how American companies liked to talk about it. "Yeah," the bosses in headquarters would say at cocktail parties in America, "we're sending Jones and Whitman over there to 'open up' China." It was as if China were a Christmas toy found hidden behind the tree, just waiting to be unwrapped and enjoyed.

In time, they would discover that scores of competitors from other countries were already inside China attacking the same gift-opening. And they would discover that China was well equipped to handle the foreigners. Nevertheless, the objective was to "open up China," like missionaries converting the unblessed.

These people from twenty-two different countries were sent to China on assignments both large and small, important and meaningless. They needed to be there, just in case this GM effort in China turned out well. What that meant to Murtaugh was that the GM operations in China were connected to a lot of other parts of General Motors, too.

In his role as general manager of GM Shanghai operations, Murtaugh reported to Rudy Schlais, president of GM China operations. Rick Swando was Murtaugh's deputy general manager. Swando, the architect of the business plan for the joint venture, did not get the top job, but he was a strong number two. He had taken on the post willingly after Jack Smith said the company wanted to bring in Murtaugh above him to run China.

"I told Jack Smith that I had no problem with that," Swando later recounted, "because Murtaugh had the manufacturing experience and understood how to build a team." So Swando reported to Murtaugh, and Murtaugh reported to Schlais. But Murtaugh was also reporting to a lot of other high-ranking people within the GM empire.

Every month, Murtaugh made the thirteen-and-a-half-hour trip from Shanghai to Detroit and listen to directives from five different GM group vice presidents. These were powerful men, presiding over large chunks of GM's burgeoning global business. All of them took home more than $1 million a year in pay, plus bonuses.

There was J. T. Battenberg III, president of the Automotive Components Group, GM's massive parts company known as ACG and later renamed Delphi. There was Donald Hackworth, group vice president of North American Truck Platforms and the man with direct control over Buick. There was Peter Hanenberger, vice president in charge of GM's global engineering standards unit in Russelsheim, Germany. There was also Louis R. Hughes, president of GM International Operations and Thomas G. Stevens, vice president and group director of Engineering Operations.

The big bosses at home knew very little about China, and China was way down the list of their priorities. Nevertheless, each had forceful, if not entirely consistent, views on how Murtaugh should take things forward in China. Murtaugh explained, "One would be saying go north, another two would tell me to head south . . . so in the end I said I'll go east."

In the corporate culture of General Motors, however, they could not let themselves be seen neglecting an initiative that was clearly so important to the CEO and the chairman. So they marched through the corporate motions, giving Murtaugh a piece of their minds while really focusing their energies on saving their own respective fiefdoms at home. They had the proverbial toe in China, just enough to say that they were "involved in the Shanghai thing" if anyone asked. But with five group vice presidents, the toes added up. Often there were just too many resources thrown at the job without much thinking behind it—like people from twenty-two different countries at a Christmas party in Shanghai.

Murtaugh's first taste of confusion surfaced not at the Christmas party but shortly after he arrived in Shanghai to start work on January 1, 1996. Another new and respected member of the team, Dieter Manthey, chief engineer from GM Opel, was making some important decisions—the kinds of decisions that normally would be made by the guy in charge.

Manthey, dispatched by Group VP Peter Hannenberger, was under the impression that he was in Shanghai to run the GM Shanghai operations.

Manthey's assumptions about his role had not materialized out of thin air. When Jack Smith took over as CEO, he immediately recognized that GM needed to "get out of Detroit" and be a much more international company. Too many decisions about markets twelve time zones away were still being taken from GM head-quarters in mid-town Detroit. The Asia-Pacific business was run by a handful of people on the sixth floor. This was problematic for many reasons.

But while the decision to "go international" was clear-cut, there was no roadmap for how to develop an international dimension to the business. Which products and which brands for which markets? There were so many brands to choose from: Chevrolet, Pontiac, Cadillac, Buick, Oldsmobile, GMC, and Saturn.

Geographic focus was another issue. GM was large and power-ful in Europe. Opel had revenues of nearly $20 billion a year and employed some forty thousand people. But future car demand would be coming from burgeoning markets in Asia—especially China—and from South America.

One of Smith's key decisions was to appoint Cleveland native Louis Hughes to the position of GM International and open an office in the "neutral" location of Geneva, Switzerland. However, Geneva proved to be too close to Russelsheim, the German head-quarters of Opel. Within a short period, a small group of people, led by Lou Hughes and Peter Hannenberger, decided that Opel would be GM's vanguard for global markets.

Clearly, in their view, German products made by German engineers would lead the charge into new markets—including China. Manthey himself had led the team that designed and engineered GM's global minivan in 1995, a product that would be sold in markets worldwide.

But the Chinese management team at SAIC had no interest in the Opel brand. They wanted the Shanghai GM venture to build and market the Buick marque, with all of its American cache and prestige. The Chinese had also heard the Germans at the Shanghai Volkswagen joint venture speaking dismissively of Opel: "Only an asshole buys an Opel" was the current expression among the Germans.

The confusion about which way to go and who was in charge reminded Murtaugh of his experiences at GM's stubbornly mediocre joint venture with Isuzu. Everyone was in charge and no one was in charge. Things did not get done.

Murtaugh decided to huddle with Hu Maoyuan, his counterpart at SAIC, and work out some basic principles for the new joint venture. After exchanging ideas, the two men presented a simple four-point set of guidelines for Shanghai General Motors. They called it the Four S's. Interestingly, Shanghai GM employees in 2010 still recited the points as if they are lines from a famous poem.

1. *Study.* The first rule for the two partners was to study and learn from one another. SAIC and GM were two powerhouse organizations developed in different languages, cultures, histories, and ownership systems. Studying was the best way to show respect for one another and to close the gap between the GM people and SAIC people.

2. *Spring.* The second rule was flexibility. Borrowing from the automotive lexicon, Murtaugh and Hu decided to refer to the springs in a car's suspension system to describe how people at Shanghai GM should think and act. They should be strong but ready to bend when it made sense; to *avoid rigidity.*

3. *Standard.* Standards and processes were the key to high quality organization. Once the company established a set of standards, all employees should respect and adhere to them.

The first three S's could probably be found in MBA textbooks and company brochures in many countries and in many languages. But the fourth S was highly unusual, especially in China:

4. *Shanghai GM.* The fourth S was the name of the 50–50 joint venture company itself. Point number four was far and away the most important S. This S said that every employee of

the joint venture should put Shanghai GM first, above all. "When you came to work for SGM, you were no longer an employee of the shareholders [SAIC or GM]," explained a veteran GM executive in 2010. "You worked exclusively for Shanghai GM."

With that simple, yet powerful four-point message, Murtaugh and Hu dared to challenge convention. They were declaring plans to build a close cooperation—a kind of cooperation never before witnessed in China's automotive industry. From the top down, all employees were required to put Shanghai GM first.

In the years that followed, Shanghai GM threw many more Christmas parties. And the number of different passports remained high. But everyone in the room pledged allegiance not to Shanghai and not to GM, but to Shanghai GM.

Murtaugh and Hu had laid down the law. It was to be Shanghai GM above all.

9

SIGNING THE DEAL

A shrill warning rippled through the phone lines of the GM China chain of command on a Sunday night in late March 1997: "If we don't have the signing on Tuesday, heads will roll!"

These clipped words were not so much a threat as a call of urgency, like sirens directing people into bomb shelters before an air attack. GM Chairman Jack Smith was coming to China to sign documents, and he had no time for disappointment.

Murtaugh's people were understandably anxious. Smith had reluctantly agreed to cancel important meetings in Detroit to make the thirteen-hour haul over the Pacific to Beijing on one condition: that he would sign the joint venture agreements with the Chinese to form Shanghai General Motors.

Confirming a meeting in China is almost never an easy thing. Signing a contract in China is never, ever, ever easy. And never, ever certain. It is a source of tremendous angst when headquarters demands certainty where none exists.

There was a certain disconnect to the urgency. It was a little like what happens to a Marine Corps candidate who, in the middle of training, feels the need to relieve himself. It's hot, the rifle is heavy, the sweat is rolling down into his eyes and he has to "go." Now! The candidate requests permission to go to the head. The platoon sergeant instructor barks back: "Request denied!"

Then the candidate starts to feel panicky. The candidate would like to ask the platoon sergeant when it will be possible to relieve himself, but he already knows what the answer will be: "When I say so, candidate—and not a moment before!"

The candidate trudges on through a forced march with constant pressure on his bladder, dreading the possibility of an accident and the mental needles of not knowing when he can get relief. It is outside of his control.

As was the signing of the Shanghai GM joint venture contract for General Motors. In spite of all of the genuine goodwill and the fact that all the terms had been agreed on, China still had the final say about when the signing would take place. And China wasn't talking. It was China's version of the Marine Corps denial of permission.

The plan seemed simple and straightforward enough. The signing ceremony was to take place on Tuesday morning in the Great Hall of the People, the massive center of power located on one side of Tiananmen Square. Jack Smith would meet with Chinese Premier Li Peng to sign the agreements and then pose for a photo session.

But it was Sunday night, Smith was already on the plane, and the Chinese officials in Beijing were still not confirming the meeting. But they were not denying the meeting either.

The issue, GM finally discovered that evening, had to do with a visit from U.S. Vice President Al Gore. By sheer coincidence, Gore planned to be in Beijing that week. He was not coming for the signing, of course. For Gore to attend a ceremony in China marking the creation of a new GM manufacturing plant would send the wrong message to the unions back in America. Unions were huge backers of the Democratic Party. In fact, the vice president's people had not been in contact with GM at all, nor had Gore and his lieutenants ever even spoken with Jack Smith.

Chinese foreign affairs officials in Beijing, on the other hand, found it extremely odd that Gore had no plans to attend the signing ceremony. Did the U.S. government not consider this joint venture important? From their point of view, it would be very poor form to have Premier Li Peng sign an agreement with the head of a U.S. company while the vice president was off visiting the Great Wall. If Gore did not feel the signing was a priority, then maybe Li Peng had better things to do with his time, too.

The GM people scrambled late into the night with U.S. State Department officials in Beijing. By dawn, they received word that

Al Gore would, in fact, be able to attend the ceremony. By midday, the Chinese government reciprocated with its own confirmation. The Tuesday morning signing event was back on, although it would not follow anything resembling the original script.

When Tuesday morning rolled around and the GM entourage arrived at the Great Hall of the People for the signing ceremony, they were instructed to wait outside the doors of the meeting room. Inside, Li Peng was already holding court with his guest, Al Gore, and the vice president's team of aides. Minutes felt like hours, and there was no indication as to when Jack Smith and his people would be allowed to enter the room, shake hands, and sign the documents.

Finally, more than an hour after the appointed time, the doors were flung open and the GM team was ushered to the front of the room. Gore and Li Peng had completed their business tête-à-tête—with no business people present. But now, at long last, GM got its shot. Smith was ushered toward Li, the two men shook hands, photos were snapped, they shook hands again. And then, just like that, it was over. The meeting with Li Peng, months in planning, was over in less than a hundred seconds.

The GM executives and their partners from Shanghai soon found themselves outside the room, stunned, wondering *What just happened?*

The next morning's *China Daily*, the national English language newspaper, featured front-page print and photos marking the historic meeting between Li Peng and Al Gore to commemorate the formation of the Shanghai GM joint venture. The GM people felt a mixture of annoyance and relief—Gore had hijacked their event, but the deal was signed.

Later that week, the mayor of Shanghai hosted a celebration dinner for Jack Smith and the new partners in Shanghai. As fate would have it, Gore's people intervened in that event too, with Secret Service personnel taking charge of the seating arrangements. At a dinner to celebrate the creation of the largest Chinese-American joint venture in history, the chairman of General Motors was not even invited to the head table. In the receiving line, people heard Tipper Gore ask her husband: "Which one is Jack Smith?"

A senior GM executive who was present in Beijing later observed wryly, "After Al Gore invented the Internet and before he decided to save the world from global warming, he hijacked GM's joint venture ceremony in China." But the congenial Jack Smith took the slights in his stride. The contracts were inked after the vice president's team left town. GM was now officially on its way in China.

Not every company operating in China can expect such dramatic intrusions, but they happen more often than one might expect. Politicians frequently visit China just so they can say that they have been to China. Once on the ground, they need some key accomplishments from their China visit for their constituents back home. Attaching themselves to an event like a sale or a joint venture in China is sure to win them more votes during the next election.

The pressure that this growing phenomenon puts on the "guys on the ground" is huge. Presidents of foreign companies operating in China, like Phil Murtaugh, are given enormous economic accountability. But in reality, they are responsible for so much more—like the ulcer-inducing, anxiety-making responsibility for managing the unforeseen intrusion of the vice president of the United States and his entourage. This task appears nowhere in the job description.

Even more stressful for frontline executives is the disconnect that exists between the expectations of the boss back at headquarters and what is realistically feasible in China. "Heads will roll" may or may not have been an exaggeration. But there is no question that when the CEO asks whether the meeting is confirmed, the blood pressure goes up and the stomach goes haywire.

What goes through the mind of the China-based executive as he considers his reply?

Yes, boss, we are doing everything within our power to secure the meeting. Everything. And I want so badly to be able to report that the meeting is confirmed that, ultimately, that's just what I'll end up doing. And then I will hold my breath. Because anyone who has ever set foot in China for more than ten days knows that nothing happens easily and no meetings are ever certain. In fact, in cases where a meeting gets confirmed in writing, days before the actual date, it means that the meeting is, ironically, really looking very doubtful. Boss, you cannot possibly imagine how things work in China.

The Chinese penchant for elusiveness—"leaving things open"—may be a strategy from the *Art of War*. Of the thirty-six strategies, Sun-Tzu reminds us, the best policy is retreat. Not retreat in the sense of surrendering or giving up. Retreat in the sense of not being visible or accessible.

Here is how it can play out in everyday work. Kerry Ivan, a former colleague of Swando, was the director of finance at the Beijing Jeep joint venture. As a CPA, Ivan knew finance like a mother knows her child. But Ivan was not too sure about his role in the joint venture, because—as is true for most joint ventures in China—there was little clarity when it came to the job.

For every manager representing the interests of the city of Beijing, there was a counterpart looking after the interests of Chrysler, the other shareholder. For example, if the position of director of marketing was held by a Chinese person, there would be a vice-director of marketing held by a foreign counterpart. Usually an American or, in Ivan's case, some non-Chinese person (Ivan hails from Australia).

Whether director or vice-director, normally you would need to secure the agreement of your counterpart on all major decisions. Normally—but it did not always work that way.

At Beijing Jeep, Li Bolin was the director of finance. Kerry Ivan was the vice-director. "At the behest of Chrysler, I was paid by the joint venture to watch the joint venture's finances," is the way Ivan explained the awkward arrangement. "My number one job was making sure BJC had the money and could pay Chrysler for the kits. Chinese LCs [letters of credit] conjured up uncertainty at the time.

"Pretty soon, I realized that we were on a 'need to know' basis. If Li Bolin, my counterpart, needed to share some information with me, then he would. Otherwise, I was on my own."

Kerry Ivan had the kind of foreign expertise that the visionaries in China's central government wanted to recruit to China. He had earned an advanced accounting degree in Australia and had managed books for every variety of company, large and small. However, he had never encountered anything like the culture and conditions at Beijing Jeep. Director Li saw Ivan as just a massive cost center and, yes, a kind of spy for American Motors. For his first year at Beijing Jeep, Ivan earned $100,000 after taxes, plus accommodations for his family at the Lido Holiday Inn, plus tuition fees for two children, plus one family R&R trip per year. Over the same 365 days, Director Li took home around 4,800rmb, then about $1,300. "The subject of my pay was never, ever mentioned by Li Bolin," said Ivan. "But everyone knew how much I and the other foreign executives made."

Every Monday morning Ivan, a strong man with thick arms and powerful hands—enduring reminders of his collegiate rugby days—would try to take notes as he joined Director Li Bolin and ten Chinese colleagues for the weekly review of the company accounts. During the meetings, Ivan would receive translations of the proceedings in bits and pieces from Ms. Zheng, his full-time assistant and interpreter. The patchy, hit-or-miss translations always left him feeling out of the loop. So one day he asked Ms. Zheng to set up a one-on-one meeting with Director Li.

Ms. Zheng marched to her desk in the corner, heels clicking on the concrete floor, and picked up her phone. They sat in opposite corners of a large office with gray walls and floors and no decor. Ms. Zheng was not in a position to call Director Li—that would be above her station—but she could contact his assistant.

"Hello, I'm from the finance department. Mr. Ivan's assistant, Little Zheng. Hello? Hello? Hello?"

Ivan saw her replace the receiver, then pick it up and try again. Same thing. Then she tried again. Finally, she reached the assistant.

She launched into a ten-minute rampage of high-pitched vocals and hand gestures, standing and grimacing and pressing her free hand against the desk top, then against the concrete wall and then to her forehead.

Ivan could not understand a word, but her body language made the call look like torture. Finally, Ms. Zheng hung up the receiver hard and stared in front of her at nothing in particular.

Ivan asked: "So, do we have an appointment with Mr. Li?"

"No. He was in a meeting."

"He was in a meeting? All that time talking and he is in a meeting?"

"Yes. He was in a meeting."

The next day, Ivan asked Ms. Zheng to try Director Li again. Once more, after getting through, she battled and clawed and growled and cajoled for ten minutes and then slammed the receiver back into cradle.

Ivan asked: "So, do we have an appointment with Mr. Li?"

"No. Director Li is at home sick today."

By the end of the second week, Ivan had developed a list, which he posted on the bare wall above his desk.

Today, Director Li is . . .

1. In a meeting.
2. At lunch.
3. Out sick.
4. On another line.
5. Called away by his boss.
6. Wife needed help with groceries.
7. Very busy today.
8. In an important meeting.
9. Not available right now.
10. At the bank.

After a while, he'd walk into the office and say: "Good morning, Ms. Zheng, how are you doing today?"

And she would respond: "Just waiting to die, Mr. Kerry."

"Okay, that's nice," he'd say.

In recounting this, Ivan commented, "I mean, I understood what she was talking about. It was miserable cold outside and indoors there was nothing but cigarette smoke and gray concrete walls."

He would again ask her to call Mr. Li for a meeting. When she hung up the phone, he would point to his list on the wall and ask her: "Okay, Ms. Zheng, which one of the reasons are we using today?"

The isolation bothered Ivan. He would spend some days "wandering around the halls counting my money and ringing the lady that did the wire transfers" just to make sure his salary would be paid on time. That's how a highly paid, seasoned finance expert spends some days in China—working very hard to confirm some basic information. The day-to-day tedium is beyond what people in the home office could ever fathom.

Planning for the visit by Jack Smith to sign the joint venture agreement had been just as tortuous. The Chinese central government was initially unresponsive. The Gore delegation came in very late and then took over the proceedings. Even the partners in Shanghai could not guarantee that the meetings in Beijing would happen.

"Don't worry," the SAIC guys had said, in an effort to comfort their new friends at GM, "we'll organize a signing event in Shanghai just for ourselves if the Beijing meeting falls through."

In the end, the planned ceremonies—in Beijing and in Shanghai—had never really taken place. But the signing had. And, in the end, that was all that mattered. "I don't care where we sign. Just so long as we get it done while Smith is in town," Murtaugh had instructed his team.

Now that the deal was finalized, it was time to get down to the enjoyable part of work: building and selling Buick Regals for the Chinese. The plant would not be fully operational for another year. But a ceremonial Job One (industry lingo for the first vehicle produced on a new assembly line) had already been planned for December, just a few months ahead.

Executing a flawless Job One would require nothing less than excellent communications between the two partners. There would be no room for the stall tactics and other mistakes the likes of which Ivan—and countless others—encountered every day in China.

10

TWO SONS

No crystal ball was needed to predict that Shanghai VW—the joint venture already well established in China—would want to test the fresh Shanghai GM romance, to throw the newcomers off balance.

But very few could have dreamt of the inventive German-Chinese arrangement that soon rattled Shanghai GM to its core.

GM's breakthrough in the spring of 1997—getting final joint venture approvals—posed a looming threat to Volkswagen. The Germans at Shanghai VW and their bosses back at Volkswagen headquarters in Wolfsburg, Germany, privately worried that GM would upend VW's perennial market leadership.

The Germans had good reason for concern. Shanghai GM was going to launch the all-new Buick Century in a state-of-the-art production facility. The tired Shanghai VW Santana, in stark contrast, was already in its twelfth year of production. Once the Buicks began surfacing in Shanghai, it would be plain to see that Volkswagen was producing relics of another era while GM was offering Chinese customers the very newest cars from America.

What's more, the Century would cater to a lucrative segment of the car market that heretofore had been met only by imports. If Shanghai GM played its cards right, it could win Chinese consumers away from the imports, away from Volkswagen—and also make a lot of money. The Century models would be selling for $40,000 or more. Profits on each car would be extremely handsome: many thousands of dollars apiece.

A senior VW executive summed up the sentiment at the time: "I really don't like the idea of Buicks running around the streets of Shanghai."

As beneficiaries of a near-monopoly, the incumbents from Germany feared the day that doors would open to competitors. But the Germans had also been operating in China long enough to understand that there was nothing they could do to stop SAIC from pursuing a new car program with GM. Both companies were partnered with SAIC. SAIC was the parent. Shanghai VW and Shanghai GM were the sons.

Yet Volkswagen executives knew they had to make a move. It seemed that VW had already played the hand dealt to it by China. The German company ran two joint ventures in China—one in the North and one with Shanghai—that captured 50 percent of the China market every year. Officials in Beijing wanted to see a little more competition.

In the face of this threat, the Germans and their Chinese partners at Shanghai VW weren't going to just sit around and wait for GM to attack. But what could be done?

In late 1997, Volkswagen entered into very quiet, very unofficial—indeed, secretive—talks with SAIC. "Would it be possible to produce a new full-size Volkswagen sedan in Shanghai?" they asked in hushed tones. And unspoken, they had a further thought: *Is there a way to build the completely redesigned VW Passat—in Shanghai?*

The talks had to be ultra-quiet for several reasons. First, General Motors would absolutely flip out if it were to learn that SAIC—its partner in the newly formed Shanghai GM joint venture—was contemplating the manufacture of a competing vehicle at Shanghai Volkswagen. Everyone understood that between 1992 and 1997 there had been a five-year bid for the rights to produce large cars for China. And GM had been the undisputed winner of that exclusive bid. Chinese approval of a second large-car program would be unconscionable.

Second, the central government would not be at all happy with such a surprise development. Premier Li Peng himself had presided over the high-profile signing of the Shanghai GM joint venture agreement. If the VW Passat were to go into production, what would stop other joint ventures in the country from clamoring to build their own large cars, too? Central government officials in Beijing had worked very hard for many years to keep the industry under control. They would not tolerate any moves to undermine their power and authority.

Despite all this, Volkswagen was determined to find out just how much power the central government really had. That's how things play out in China. The first rule of operating successfully in China is to learn the government's plan. And there is *always* a plan. It may not be concise or even clear, but a plan always exists. The second rule is to make a judgment as to how far the plan will stray from its original form into something entirely different.

Plans, policies, regulations—all are definitely open to shaping by people and events on the ground. There is the plan, which takes form as a policy. Then there is the reality, which is often something completely outside of either the plan or the policy.

China's car industry had been planned from the outset. The central government visionaries wanted to build an auto industry around a handful of powerful manufacturers, like the Big Three in Detroit or the Big Six in Japan (Toyota, Nissan, Honda, Mitsubishi, Isuzu, and Suzuki), as they were known in the day. To get there, China's major municipalities would partner with only the world's best carmakers.

The original aim was to lure GM, Ford, Toyota, and Nissan into joint ventures. And then China would again close its doors. With time and protection, the Chinese partners would learn the industry from their global partners and soon be able to produce cars that the Chinese could call their own.

That was the plan. The reality that played out was that, in the mid-1990s, China found itself partnered with the global automotive equivalent of ninety-eight-pound weaklings. American Motors, Volkswagen, Peugeot, and Citroën were all on shaky ground financially, and their competitiveness in the marketplace was in serious doubt.

Although up to that point the Chinese plan had failed to attract the best and brightest automakers, it had at least kept an orderly arrangement of producers. The industry was tightly regulated, and each joint venture was given a segment in which it was allowed to grow its business. The Chinese planners, inspired by engineering backgrounds, went so far as to divvy up the market into segments determined by each car's engine size, as depicted in the table.

Approved Car Segments in China, 1997	
Engine Size	Make and Model
1.1–.1.3 liters	Daihatsu Charade
1.4 liters	Citroën ZX
1.6 liters	Volkswagen Jetta
1.8 liters	Volkswagen Santana
2.0 liters	Peugeot 505
2.2 liters	Audi 100
2.5–3 liters	Buick Century

The policy makers in Beijing had held the line and been quite thoughtful when it came to market segmentation. This ensured that each joint venture had its own sandbox to play in. But, to their chagrin, the absence of a modern car continued to stimulate the smuggling of imports. So it had been decided that China's new national large-car manufacturer, Shanghai General Motors, would have exclusive rights to supply the market for cars with engine sizes between 2.5 and 3 liters.

The nearest competitor to Buick's new large-car entrant, the Audi 100, was actually a bit of a mutant that was produced only in China. It featured the chassis and body parts of the Audi 100, a car that had already been phased out of production in the West. And strangely, the car was powered by a 2.2-liter gasoline engine designed and engineered by Chrysler Corporation. (Imagine the Germans' bruised sensibilities when they witnessed the proud, albeit dated, Audi sedan powered by an American engine!) The Chinese had acquired the Chrysler engine line in a separate negotiation and figured that they could save money by building a German-American blended car.

Now, the official blessing for Shanghai GM to build Buicks threatened to upset Volkswagen's long-held position of market dominance.

Volkswagen had just launched an upgraded version of the Santana: the Santana 2000. It had a longer wheelbase than the original

Santana (offering more backseat legroom) and also featured power windows and ABS brakes as standard. But at its core it was still very much the original Santana. Worse, even the newly updated Santana 2000 would look old next to the Buick coming from GM.

Shanghai Volkswagen understood that it must retain its edge in product. And that meant it must bring a new product to China.

Most worrisome to Volkswagen was the risk that GM would spellbind and charm SAIC, just as a younger minor wife threatens the position of the incumbent first wife. Would SAIC begin to favor GM over Volkswagen when it came to personnel decisions or political influence?

Executives at VW coveted GM's abilities when it came to the "soft" talents of marketing and public relations. Privately, they said that if Volkswagen only possessed GM's abilities in marketing, there was no doubt that the German company could match or better any brand in the world—even the vaunted Toyota.

While Volkswagen worried that GM might charm SAIC in order to gain certain advantages, they concluded that it was pointless to fret about things they could not control. What Volkswagen *could* control was product. Even with the old Santana, Volkswagen had earned some grudging respect from the Chinese management at SAIC. In the eyes of the Chinese, the Germans—unlike the French or the Italians—were "serious" professionals when it came to the art of shaping metal and electronics into sturdy, no-nonsense cars.

The question for VW, then, was how to ease the Passat through the arduous China approvals process without attracting notice—and emphatic objections from GM and from the central government.

There were two core elements of the German strategy. The first was to remind SAIC about the fruits of their partnership since 1985. The Volkswagen Santana, produced in Shanghai, had been the nation's number one seller every year since the formation of the Shanghai Volkswagen joint venture in 1984. It routinely led the market and was easily the best choice among a limited range of models available to buyers in China during the 1980s and early 1990s. "Volkswagen" in German means "people's car"— and Santana had become the people's car of China.

There is a Chinese adage that describes what's necessary in life in four characters:

衣　　食　　住　　行

Yi (clothes)　*Shi* (food)　*Zhu* (home)　*Xing* (travel)

So ubiquitous were VWs on the road that the company ran a corporate advertisement, to wide acclaim, that inserted the VW logo in place of the Chinese character for travel. VW was a permanent fixture on Chinese roads. The Shanghai VW partnership had been a real winner. So it was in everyone's interest—was it not?—to allow that winner a new product.

The second aspect of the Shanghai VW strategy was to avoid coming right out and identifying the new product as a Passat, which—based on its size and features—would have been seen as an obvious competitor with the Buick Century. Instead, they referred to the proposed car as either the engineering code name B5 or the "next-generation Santana."

By not referring to the Passat by name, Shanghai VW could approach the central government for approval to build the model while offering the officials in Beijing some wiggle room on interpretation. It helped, too, that the Passat would be powered by a 2.0 liter engine, which—at least on paper—separated it from the Buick.

This "correct naming of things" or "correct presentation of things" is one of the core features of Chinese culture. So long as you set up your words in a way that appears palatable, anything is possible.

Perhaps the best example of this correct naming of things comes from the normalization of relations between the United States and China in 1979. For years, a sticking point between the two nations was how to treat the sensitive question of Taiwan. The United States wished to preserve the independence of Taiwan—its ally since 1949. The Chinese vehemently rejected any suggestion of Taiwan's independence. There seemed to be no way to work around the conflicting priorities.

But then the U.S. team developed a wording that said, in effect, *there is only one China, and Taiwan is part of China.* The U.S. wording omitted mention of whether the government of Taiwan or the communist party in Beijing was the legitimate ruler of China.

In that way, U.S. recognition of Taiwan's independence was implicitly preserved, while China was satisfied that the "renegade province" did not enjoy official U.S. acknowledgment of its status as a sovereign nation.

VW's use of the "correct naming" strategy worked. VW eventually won quiet approval to build the Passat in Shanghai. There was no formal announcement; instead, the news leaked out to the industry, and to GM, in the form of a rumor.

In the spring of 1998, a delegation of senior executives from leading component makers in Europe visited the headquarters of Shanghai Volkswagen. The German head of production presented all of the relevant capacity and production numbers for the year. Then he gave some indications of the production volumes over the next three years to 2000. There was a marked jump in the projected numbers, which prompted one of the visitors to raise his hand with a question: "What explains the large increase in production over the next few years?"

"There will be increased production of the Santana and the Santana 2000," replied the German in a matter-of-fact, stating-the-obvious tone.

One of the Chinese managers from Shanghai VW was helping to translate from German into English. As interpreters often do, he decided to add his own color to the explanation: "There will be the Santana, the Santana 2000, and the, um, the B5," he finished with some gusto.

"The B5? What is the B5?" the now very curious component maker asked, leaning forward on the boardroom table.

"B5. You know, the B5. It's the all-new Volkswagen Passat. We are working with suppliers now to get ready for production."

Huh? There was a prolonged silence in the room as minds began to race. Was it conceivable that Volkswagen would produce the Passat in China? There had been no official announcement, no invitation to bid, no change in policy. No, there must be some mistake. How could Volkswagen be planning to build the Passat, which would be a direct and formidable competitor to the Buicks soon to be produced by Shanghai GM?

"You are going to build the Passat here in Shanghai?" the European executive pressed once more.

"The B5, yes. We're preparing the Passat," said the Chinese manager, with a nervous glance toward the German boss.

This was stunning news, delivered in a most unconventional way.

Word of the new Passat shot like lightning across town to the GM headquarters. How could Volkswagen be allowed to build the Passat? Everyone knew that the large-car program had been awarded exclusively to GM.

Not believing the rumors—wanting desperately not to believe them—senior GM executives approached the SAIC team with the story.

"We have heard some strange rumors that Volkswagen is going to make the Passat here. This cannot be true. You know that car is in direct competition with our Buick."

As if well prepared for the visit, the Chinese executive from SAIC replied matter-of-factly, "It's like this. Imagine you have two sons. You just can't give something to one son without also allowing the same for the second one."

With those simple and pithy words, SAIC demolished GM's hopes for a large-car segment monopoly in China.

But . . . what about all of the time and money and effort that had been poured into the long, painful bidding process? And what about the promise of segment exclusivity? Did they not call Shanghai GM China's national large-car program?

All of that is true and genuine, the SAIC officials acknowledged. But what can you do when you have two sons?

Rewind a bit. After months of secret negotiations, the executives from Volkswagen have just obtained the approval for production of the new Passat in China. Only now do they feel confident enough to relax a little and snicker about their (still unsuspecting) rivals at GM.

At the end of a hard week of work at the Shanghai Volkswagen plant in Anting, they gather in the Paulaner Bierhaus and disparage their new crosstown competitors.

"There are only two things on earth visible from the moon," they say, raising tall glasses of weissbier to a collective clink. "One is the Great Wall. And the other—the other are the gaps in GM cars."

In the industry, the term "gaps" refers to wide or uneven spaces between the body parts of a car, like where the hood meets the front quarter panel. Too much of a gap demonstrates a lack of attention to detail—a sign of poor quality. The Germans judge GM products as inferior, particularly when it comes to anything that requires precision.

GM had assumed that its triumph over Ford would give the company exclusive rights to produce all the vehicles for China's large-car segment. But as they had quickly learned, there was a wide gap between that very reasonable assumption and the reality of their new venture in China. And that gap would only grow wider.

PART THREE

NEGOTIATING THE OBSTACLE COURSE

11

THE LAUNCH

The jolting news that the Volkswagen Passat was soon going to be built across town was tough for GM to take, no matter what SAIC's explanation might be. The entire premise of the General Motors investment in the "national luxury car program" in Shanghai was that Buick would be the exclusive product to rid China of those pesky imported luxury cars, once and for all.

Research in early 1998 had shown that around 120,000 imports a year were still finding their way into China by the cover of night or by the shadow of government or military agencies in the South. The Shanghai GM plant was designed to build 100,000 cars per year. Although the new Buick would still have to contend with some imports—they would not go away overnight—if Shanghai GM could manage to displace more than half of the imports in the first year, then the venture would be off to a great start.

But with Passat entering the picture, Shanghai GM would have to compete against both the imports and Shanghai VW. It was especially hard to swallow the fact that the Passat was going to be built in partnership with SAIC. When the Shanghai municipality instructed its agencies to buy "local," purchases would now be divided between the Buick Century and the Volkswagen Passat. This was critical, because government agencies and state enterprises were still accounting for 80 percent of car purchases in China.

There was more bad news. The Guangzhou-Peugeot joint venture, established in 1986, had caved under pressure from the imports and filed bankruptcy in 1997. That was not a surprise. The real blow came in July 1998, when it was announced that

Honda Motor Company was forming a new 50–50 joint venture with Guangzhou Automobile Corp. (GAC); it is now known as Guangzhou Automobile Group (GAG). Honda would refurbish the old Peugeot plant in order to launch a new model—the Honda Accord! The knife was twisted with the announcement that Honda was planning to invest only a paltry $125 million dollars in this Chinese effort.

Since the early 1990s, Honda Accord imports had grown extremely popular among Chinese consumers, especially in Guangdong Province. Officials at GAC went to Beijing and said, "Look, we are doing our part to reduce Japanese imports. Now Honda will make their cars inside China—with us!"

GAC enjoyed another kind of leverage. As the largest provincial contributor to national tax coffers, Guangdong often received special treatment from officials in Beijing. Shanghai did not like it, but the powerful city had no way to block the tax-paying, import-substituting Guangzhou Automobile Corp. Besides, GAC would argue, the Honda Accord was not a new program. It was simply replacing the (failed) Peugeot 505 business.

In the space of less than a year, Shanghai GM's "monopoly" on the large car market in China had evaporated. Now the 120,000-car market would be divided among gray-market imports, Passats, Accords, and Buicks. The Accord was already a perennial best seller in America, routinely trouncing Buick in its own backyard. If Buick could not compete in America, how would it hope to prevail against Honda and Volkswagen in China?

Not ready to throw in the towel, Phil Murtaugh and his team at Shanghai GM needed to buckle down and find a way to sell more Buicks. It was still several months before the cars would begin flowing into the marketplace, so the team focused most of its attention on the plant, putting systems in place to ensure that the Buicks were of the highest quality.

The City of Shanghai had earlier set an aggressive timeline for Shanghai GM to start production in 1998. But in the fall of that year, it was plain to see that the plants and the suppliers would not be ready until April of 1999. Nevertheless, the City insisted on "an event" before the end of 1998.

In the car industry, Job One events—such as the first car off the assembly line—are an opportunity to show off the results of years of hard work by thousands of people. The day carries a special significance, like a baby's baptism, a Sweet Sixteen party, or any other tradition that marks the beginning of a grand future. You want everything to go exactly according to plan.

Invitations were sent to top media, ranking government officials, the chief executives of supplier companies, and other friends of GM and the City of Shanghai. Throughout the morning there would be plant tours, speeches by the leading executives, and lots of people shooting film and taking photos. But the main event, the centerpiece of these celebrations, is always when the big bosses get into the first car and drive it off the line.

On this day, the big bosses were Jack Smith, chairman and CEO of General Motors, and Xu Kuangdi, mayor of Shanghai. After they climbed in and closed the doors of the gleaming white Buick Century—with Smith in the driver's seat and Xu as the front seat passenger—a crowd of two thousand people waited anxiously for the car to make its debut, rolling off the line and onto the factory floor, ready for the first Chinese customer.

And wait they did. The car fired up, but did not move. There was a bit of delay and then a plunking sound. There was movement— not of the car moving forward, but of the hood popping open. While searching for the emergency brake release, Smith had inadvertently pulled the hood release.

The brand new Buick Century for China, Job One, stood motionless for long, awkward seconds with its hood agape for all to see. Smith recovered quickly (with the help of some factory hands nearby), found the brake release, and guided the car forward without further incident. The popped hood episode would be an inauspicious sign anywhere, but the Chinese can be especially superstitious.

A magnanimous and affable man, Smith handled the scene well, laughing it off and allowing everyone else to join in with their own nervous chuckles. "You don't use that brake in America," he said. But the popped hood served to water some seeds of worry that had been planted in the minds of the Chinese leaders at Shanghai GM. They had heard that GM was a giant bureaucracy, not in touch with its consumers or even its own products. To see the top boss from General Motors fumble around with the parking brake almost certainly reinforced their doubts and suspicions.

Phil Murtaugh was not the superstitious type. He was a guy who was interested in getting things done—in results. He considered most formal events to be distractions, at best.

In early 1999, Murtaugh was asked to play host to a group of American journalists at a five-star hotel restaurant in Shanghai. The event had been arranged by GM's public relations people, and every last detail, including the seating arrangements, had been choreographed to go "just right." Murtaugh took a seat at the middle of the table and, after a few uncomfortable moments, leaned over to the veteran journalist next to him and said, "I really hate these formal lunches." The journalist laughed out loud and nodded in agreement.

Murtaugh had a way of saying such things in a matter-of-fact way that was both abrupt and disarming. A GM executive who was more at home in a manufacturing plant, Murtaugh was intensely interested in making Buick a success in China. The Job One ceremony was a necessary event, but to Murtaugh it was nothing more than a high-profile ritual that must be conducted in order to get down to the real business of building cars.

Like everyone else, Murtaugh was uncertain what kind of demand the Buick Century would generate. He understood that marketing and selling every new Buick car in China would be a battle. Regulators would change the rules without notice— introducing new safety or emissions standards, or granting special subsidies to certain Chinese companies. And competitors would be working to take advantage of every misstep at Shanghai GM.

He counted on help from his partner, SAIC, to reach the first-year sales goal. Unlike America, where there is a strong inclination to view government as an obstacle to progress, the City of Shanghai government was a true partner. So it takes some rethinking to understand that in China, the government is often the business and the business is often the government. The traditional lines are blurred. In Shanghai GM's case, it was in everyone's interest to achieve the sales the goal. And the City had enough political muscle to instruct its constituents on what to buy.

Although SAIC is a Fortune 500 company, its chairman is, first and foremost, a member of the Communist Party; second, a government official; and third—almost incidentally—a business executive. The difference between such an executive and his peers from the West is that American business executives view the world primarily through a prism first of money, then of power. The Chinese leader tends to see the world the other way around. "[Doing] business is a kind of temporary sideshow for them as they move up the Party ranks," explained a former Chinese automotive executive and Party member.

Heading into their first year of production in 1999, executives at General Motors felt hopeful about the prospects for success. They were getting ready to assemble the most modern car ever made on Chinese soil. The new Buick Century offered many best-in-class safety and comfort features, including, notably, the first ever made-in-China automatic transmission. The Shanghai GM manufacturing plant was by far the most modern in the country.

When Chinese government officials bought cars, they invariably bought the color black. Black in China is the color of power. Riding in a black American sedan would be the ultimate projection of clout. During a Shanghai GM plant tour in the spring of 1999, the manager in charge of engine production was asked the percentage of black Buicks out of all that were going out the door. "Eighty percent," he said without hesitation.

The ratio of black cars was good news and bad news for Murtaugh. The good news was that the City was clearly committed to helping the joint venture make its first-year sales target. "We started making cars [at the joint venture] in April, and by July we were already profitable," Murtaugh would recount later. But the majority of orders for black sedans caused some worry. The heavy percentage of black Buicks indicated that private buyers— the exact segment of the car-buying population that Shanghai GM had hoped to capture—were not buying many Buicks.

A comparison with Honda was revealing. Honda had started making its Chinese Accord in 1999. The majority of Hondas on the road were white, silver, or metallic gray—colors favored by private buyers. There were black Accords, too. But the color preferences of Accord buyers indicated that it was the Japanese, not Shanghai GM, who were getting out in front with private buyers.

In 1999, Shanghai GM sold twenty thousand Buick Centurys and Honda sold just over ten thousand Accords. Buick had beaten

Honda, two to one. But Honda had invested only a fraction of what GM had poured into China. And Honda had purposely *limited* sales to ten thousand in the first year—it could have sold many more. By the end of 1999, the average waiting period for a new Accord buyer in China was more than ten months! Honda's ability to persuade customers to wait such a long time for their new car revealed the underlying strength of the brand.

But the extended wait was also a strategic move by Honda that would seem to run counter to common sense. Honda purposely limited production volumes and cultivated longer waiting periods. They had been selling cars to Chinese customers, via the Hong Kong import channels, since the early 1990s; they understood a quirky dimension of the Chinese consumer's psyche. For Chinese buyers, the length of time required to get your hands on a product can indicate a level of value. Chinese consumers tend to avoid or look askance at products that are too readily available.

Conversely, Chinese consumers demonstrate astonishing willingness to wait for a product that is perceived to be of superior value. The longer the wait, the better. Among Chinese consumers today, the most sought-after women's luxury bags are the ones that cost a lot *and* feature a waiting list.

Honda's long waiting lists puzzled Shanghai GM. The Japanese brand's success did not make intuitive sense. "What's Honda up to?" Murtaugh's lieutenants would ask their wide retinue of contacts in the industry at the time.

In 2000, Buick Century sales climbed to thirty thousand cars. But on an annualized basis that was only slightly higher than the twenty thousand sold in 1999 after production began in April. Worse than that, Honda managed to sell thirty-two thousand Accords. And even worse, VW sold thirty thousand Passats, despite their later arrival to the market. In terms of momentum, Accord and Passat were on the upswing, while Buick was faltering. In 2001, both the Accord and the Passat would sell more than fifty thousand cars, while sales of the Century slumped to twenty thousand.

There had to be some good reasons why the Buick Century was not selling better. But determining the root cause was difficult. Traditional market research was often unreliable or incomplete.

Because the car buyers were mostly government agencies, it was necessary to interview the purchasing departments, the drivers, and the people riding in the car.

Researchers could usually get access to the purchasing agents. But they would indicate that the decision was in the hands of the higher-ups in the organization, the kinds of people who had no time to meet with market researchers.

Here's an excerpt of a report from Timothy Dunne, at the time a partner at the consultancy Automotive Resources Asia:

> Lining up interviews with car buyers has been a challenge. You can't just call up a company and request an interview—people are either confused by the request or suspicious of your motives. We had to do it the Chinese way, with *guanxi* and going the indirect route. That involves having staff call their friends who might know someone, who might know someone, who has a friend, a classmate, or a father or an uncle or some other relation that works in the vehicle department of a company. Then they might, maybe, agree to an interview.
>
> The airport at Shenyang—a city of five million people—was an old airport hangar. The entry "doors" of the airport/hangar consisted of thick plastic strips (oily and dusty) hung from a garage-door-like opening that all the passengers had to pass through. Inside the hangar, there were concrete floors, little lighting, no heat (it was about 35 degrees outside) and no conveyor belts. Our luggage was wheeled in on carts through the same door that the passengers had used. Then it was a scrum to get your luggage: Lots of shouting and pushing and pulling and elbows flying as people tried to get their bag first.
>
> We had our first meeting at an affiliate of the CACC (China's state-owned airline organization). We pulled into the courtyard of the office building where the meeting was to be held. Wei Yan went in first to find our contact, and then we were directed to the back of building, where the company's fleet of two dozen cars was kept in a large garage.
>
> We went into an adjacent one-story office building, where a half-dozen drivers were sitting around in a small reception room on tattered and greasy sofas and chairs situated around a wooden table. All the drivers were dressed in coats and hats—still no heat—and the room was filled with smoke from heavy Chinese cigarettes, and the aroma of hot tea. The table was

covered with a half dozen overflowing ashtrays and used teacups. Everyone was friendly. We were given seats, and offered tea and cigarettes.

After introductions, we started with our questions. They walked us through how purchase decisions were made. Basically, the company's general manager would be told his vehicle budget for the year, and he made all the decisions. The budget was to cover new vehicle purchases, plus maintenance of the existing fleet (oil changes, new tires, spare parts, etc.) and operating costs (gas) for the entire fleet. The drivers handled all maintenance responsibilities (that's where all the grease on the sofas came from, I assume).

These field reports were colorful and fascinating, but they did not deliver the kind of precise market research that marketers at GM were accustomed to getting back in America. What Shanghai GM could count on is how the Chinese media described Buick, over and over again:

1. Good Points: Big, Strong, and Safe
2. Bad Point: Gas Guzzler

Big, strong, and safe are all great attributes. But they would have a tough time overcoming "gas guzzler." The Chinese are ready to spend top dollar on a car. But it really annoys them to frequently return to the gas pump to have their pocketbooks drained.

The Accord and the Passat each came with 2-liter, 4-cylinder engines. The Century was powered by a 3-liter, V6 engine. Acceleration and passing power, things that matter a lot to American drivers, did not count for much in China. The Chinese wanted a vehicle with a great image taking them in comfort from Point A to Point B. But they would not spend one penny more than necessary on gas.

The engineers at the Buick division in America had already reduced the size of the engine once to qualify for the Shanghai large-car program. They could not fathom making the engine smaller again. "You just don't put a damn four-cylinder engine into a Buick," they said. That would instantly transform the Buick into a "dog"—a reference to how slowly a large car powered by a small engine would move when the traffic light turns green. Dogs were bad. Dogs could ruin careers at General Motors. Plus, changing the size of the engine would take money and time and people.

But the fact remained that the Century was under tremendous pressure from Passat and Accord, plus the still-continuing gray channel imports. So Shanghai GM looked at other ways to win customers. In its quest to revolutionize the business of making and selling cars in China, the company had set very high standards in one area that competitors in China had largely neglected: car dealerships.

Before GM arrived, China did not have conventional car dealerships. If a customer was in the market for a new car, he had one of two options.

The most common way to buy a car was to travel straight to the factory. Car buyers were dispatched from their work units—primarily state-owned enterprises and government agencies. Their job was to drive cars for the higher-ups in the government agencies. While they had driver's licenses, most of them never dreamed of owning and driving their own car. Getting from the company to the factory to pick up a new car and back could take three or four days. Buyers would carry a suitcase full of cash from their place of work to the factory gates. They usually traveled in twos to thwart potential robbers. Buyers exchanged giant stacks of bills (even in 2011, China's largest note is 100 yuan—a little more than $15, depending on the exchange rate) for new cars.

As a second option, buyers could go to massive open-air parking lots on the outskirts of large cities like Beijing where all brands and models were parked side by side. There, rain or shine, you would find Toyotas next to Jeeps next to Fords next to Suzukis next to Peugeots.

These parking lots were like a giant physical eBay for car customers. Buyers would negotiate the price with one of the dozens of brokers who wandered among the cars, settle in cash, and then drive away. To the Chinese, buying a car was just a transaction; little different from buying a loaf of bread.

Most cars were covered with a thin layer of dust, an odd sign to Chinese buyers that the car was genuinely brand-new. "You'll be the first to lay your hands on this beauty—not even the dust has been removed, you see?"

Shanghai GM saw an opportunity to distinguish the Buick brand from all others in the market by building a first-class network of car dealers and service stations. To get there, they borrowed heavily from the successes of the Saturn brand in the United States, where the buying and service experience was designed to be as friendly as possible. At Saturn, there was no price haggling, and when people came to pick up their cars there was a small celebration in the show-room that coincided with delivery of the car. Shanghai GM aimed to duplicate that effective and satisfying experience in China.

Shanghai GM's management convinced dealers to invest mil-lions of dollars to make the Buick showrooms the finest and most advanced in the industry. The dealerships featured expensive floor-to-ceiling glass, highly trained sales and service personnel, and state-of-the-art ordering and logistics systems.

The executives at Shanghai GM understood that the people coming to buy the cars would be, for the most part, not the actual driver-owners. But Shanghai GM was certain that, in the coming years, more and more private individuals would have the money to buy their own cars. And they would grow fondly attached to the Buick dealership experience.

A great overall experience keeps the customer coming back for parts and service. That was the secret to the meteoric rise of Lexus in America. The car was superb, but Lexus really made a difference when it came to treating their customers with care and respect. "It's not just the car," a Lexus executive later explained to a group of Chinese journalists. "The whole ownership experience is the key to success."

That's a little like saying that the Apple iPhone is all about the Genius Bar, the place where owners get service for their Apple products. The creative moniker "Genius Bar" is a beautiful improve-ment over the boring "service desk" tag. But users go to the Genius Bar only after purchasing the product, the iPhone.

Whether we are talking about mobile phones or cars, there is no escaping the fact that the product is king. Car owners point to their shiny new car in the driveway, not to their neat service record book in the glove compartment.

Shanghai GM was selling enough cars for the factory to turn a profit. But the newly minted Buick dealers had invested big money, with the expectation that Buicks would be flying out the front door. That was not happening.

The dealers were growing very impatient. "The dealers were getting so they wouldn't listen to us [anymore]—it was bad," recalled an executive who worked on network development at the time. Murtaugh and his team needed to find a way to increase sales in a hurry.

international expansion when the Chinese refuse to embrace the obvious superiority of the "made in Germany" engine?

More than likely, the Chinese opted for the push-rod engine not because the overhead cam from Germany "was no better," but because the Chinese at SAIC saw the choice of engines as a kind of political litmus test. If SAIC executives chose the German engine, they might end up offending the Americans with whom they were negotiating the joint venture. Better to keep cultivating a tight relationship with the Americans, even if it meant not having the very best engine.

Several members of the SAIC team had previous experience working with the German engineers at Volkswagen. It was no secret that the Chinese preferred the "open and flexible" (or was it, perhaps, easier, more lenient?) approach that the Americans brought to the joint venture talks. For the German engineers at Opel, there could be only one explanation: because their American colleagues at Buick could not outdo them in technology, they instead had outmaneuvered them in the political arena.

The Germans at GM Opel were not ready for a complete surrender, however. They would find a way to make their mark. Sooner or later, they believed, engineering excellence would catapult Opel to the front in China.

They got another shot when it came time to choosing a welding process for the new Shanghai GM plant. In recognition of their engineering prowess, Opel had been appointed GM's global "lead" when it came to significant engineering decisions at new plants. As such, a team of Opel engineers took up position in Shanghai to determine the best processes at the new plant.

The Germans from Opel had one point of view. The American engineers from Buick in North America had a different point of view. In this case, it happened that the American process was more involved, because it featured extra steps to protect the body panels from rust. The German approach was simpler and more efficient, but it did not offer heavy-duty protection against corrosion.

The people who developed new cars at Buick headquarters in Michigan always prescribed double-sided electro-galvanized sheet metal. The two sides provided an extra layer of protection against corrosion caused by salt. It was common practice for city trucks to dump generous amounts of salt on Detroit streets to get ice and snow to melt. In Germany, the engineers for Opel cars always mandated single-sided electro-galvanized sheet metal because they did not have any direct experience with salt.

This battle was as much about turf as it was about technology. The Opel Technical Development Center (TDC) was given global authority to determine manufacturing processes, including those for the new plant in Shanghai. The North American Engineering Center took charge of vehicle design for GM cars, including the Buick Century.

The German team on site in Shanghai specified the more basic sheet metal welding process. But to meet the car design requirements, the plant needed a process called "dual pulse" welding, whereby, as explained by a senior executive at GM China at the time, the "weld guns clamp the metal and a very short high current pulse is sent through the guns to blow away the galvanizing. Then comes a longer, slightly cooler pulse to weld together the base metals."

The Germans insisted that the new plant adopt their simpler process. This time they held their ground and eventually reached a standoff with their engineering counterparts back in Michigan. Things were stuck. Time was wasting away. That's when a meeting was convened and Murtaugh "screamed at [the Germans] and told them that if they did not put in the dual-pulse welding, [he] would be sending them all back to Germany," an executive in the meeting later recalled.

Turf wars arise in companies all over the world. What made these battles in Shanghai significant was that, for the first time, the GM clashes were occurring in a car market that would one day become the world's largest. And the battles were taking place in plain view of GM's partner and ultimate competitor, SAIC.

The Chinese began to understand that, with GM, you had what amounted to companies operating within companies, leading to divisive competition for the final word. This time it was the Opel welding process versus the Buick North American welding process. Previously it had been Opel engines versus Buick engines. And at times it looked like the ground rules at GM were *every man for himself.*

Buick, a brand for the gray-haired in America, was fast becoming GM's thoroughbred in China. Opel, the cultivator of some of the best technologies in the company, had become little more than an also-ran. Imagine, then, Opel's delight when the Shanghai GM team first expressed an interest in the Opel Corsa for China. The Opel ticket to the China market had finally arrived!

Executives at Opel quickly "pulled a Blagojevich," as one former GM executive later described it. That term refers to the former governor of Illinois who tried, without success, to trade favors for a U.S. Senate seat that was left open when Barack Obama became president of the United States in 2008. As governor of Illinois, Blagojevich had authority to appoint the new senator. The U.S. Senate seat "is a f***ing valuable thing," Blagojevich was recorded saying at that time. "You just don't give it away for nothing." (Blagojevich's actual word choice will be recalled by those who read it in the published transcripts.)

The Germans at Opel had their Blagojevich opening: "You, over there in China, don't just get the Opel Corsa from Germany for nothing. We don't just give it away." The Opel Corsa could and should go to China, they said, provided the product retained its Opel brand name. To them, there was no sense in sending an Opel to China and calling it anything but an Opel. Of course, having an Opel-badged Corsa in China would open the door to more Chinese customers buying other Opel models in the future. And more power for Opel managers worldwide.

Executives in charge of strategy at headquarters in Detroit had a different idea. For them, the number one priority was to tidy up GM's brands in overseas markets. Their recommendation was to have Chevrolet as the main GM brand in new markets. One set of voices in headquarters had decreed Opel as the lead for new markets. A second set of voices wanted Chevrolet to be the consistent GM brand, regardless of where the product came from. Making Chevrolet the lead brand for new markets also made sense because it was GM's largest and strongest division and it made cars for the middle class.

When it came to branding the Opel Corsa in China, Murtaugh listened carefully to the arguments from the Opel crowd and the

Chevrolet crowd. Then he politely but firmly threw both arguments out the window.

Ever the pragmatist, Murtaugh needed a simple, workable solution. Presenting the Opel Corsa to Chinese consumers as a Buick was not the ideal solution, he understood. But Shanghai GM had a network of hungry Buick dealers. The joint venture had already invested close to $50 million to build awareness of the Buick brand in China. The Buick dealers had poured in tens of millions of dollars of their own, and they needed new products—now.

Shanghai GM had worked hard to cultivate an image of exclusivity and power for Buick. Making a small, affordable car for the emerging middle class under the Buick name ran counter to that lofty positioning. The new car would be a Buick—"a Buick in a smaller package," Murtaugh said with conviction, and left it at that.

When it came to tough calls, the right call would be the one that put the joint venture in the best possible position for success. The goal was not to placate the Opel Division. Nor was it to kowtow to the powerful executives who recommended corporate strategy from the Detroit headquarters. The goal was to make Shanghai GM strong and profitable. Murtaugh needed a product for his Buick dealers, and it made no sense to spend tens of millions of dollars on a second brand before getting the first one right.

The early priority that Rudy Schlais, recently promoted to president of GM Asia Pacific operations, had placed on making the joint venture a success had deeper implications for Murtaugh. The foreign and Chinese partners in the other car joint ventures— Beijing Jeep, Shanghai Volkswagen—had different goals. There was constant conflict. Each partner had an eye on making money at the expense of the other partner. It was a zero-sum game.

Making the joint venture a success meant that Murtaugh could place Shanghai GM, the company for which he had profit and loss responsibility, first in line. Schlais made it clear that Murtaugh did not have to worry about the parent company (GM) so long as he made the joint venture grow and prosper.

This was not how things usually worked. Normally, an executive on the front lines in China would be expected to both satisfy the parent *and* make the joint venture thrive. This left frontline executives vulnerable to all kinds of potential blame and recrimination should things go wrong:

- The guy missed the market.
- The guy pissed off the Chinese partners.
- The guy screwed up the branding.
- The guy left too much money on the table.

Rick Swando summed it up like this: There was a very real risk (that is, before Schlais' arrival) for anyone working in China to be "left twisting in the wind" at the first sign of adversity. Yesterday's supporters would scatter like rats, leaving the man in charge to fend for himself. A perfectly crafted career at GM could come crashing down because word would spread within the company that "the guy over in China had made a mess of things." That was how one came to the unhappy fate of being "left twisting in the wind."

This is one of the great untold secrets of life as a foreign executive sent on assignment to China. He comes into the position steeled for a bruising fight with competitors and regulators in China's ever changing and unpredictable market. And he gets one. But this rocky and uncertain road is rendered even more difficult to negotiate by the draining battles to get people at your own company back home to understand the simplest things. Like, for example, the urgency of bringing in another Buick to complement the Century.

It seemed that top managers in headquarters could understand such needs only when the requested move aligned neatly with the stars in their own universe of priorities. For many back in the home office, China was still a market just this side of Mars. With the blessing from Schlais, however, Murtaugh could make the (imperfect) decision to put Opels under Buick badges.

So it was decided. Shanghai GM would begin production of the Opel Corsa in December, 2000. The car would be called the Buick Sail. It would also have a Chinese name, Sai-Ou, which translates as "Compete-Europe." The Chinese name was a quiet tribute to the product's German roots and a less-subtle jab at its cross-town rival, Volkswagen.

Phil Murtaugh had his small car to feed his hungry dealers. But the drawn-out process of searching for and then negotiating the rights to brand the new car for China had uncovered an even bigger problem. A discovery so big that you would call it not a problem, but a disaster: General Motors, the world's number one producer of vehicles, did not make the kinds of products that Chinese people wanted.

The Buick Century might sell in fair numbers to government officials who were spending state budgets—but not those spending their own money. And the private buyers would cringe at every trip to the gas station as they watched the numbers on the pump spin beyond their wallets. Buick's 3-liter engine had a reputation for gulping gasoline.

The Buick Sail was a temporary bandage necessary to patch the fresh wounds of Chinese dealers. But without the means to make affordable small products, what would Shanghai GM do next?

13

PAPER CUPS

How do you create a product that the Chinese will embrace in great numbers? Shanghai GM was faced with this pressing question as it endeavored to design and build cars that offered American size, safety, and exclusivity without too much engine and too high a price. And there was no time to miscalculate or get it wrong again.

At least part of the answer was unfolding right before their eyes in China.

Starting in the early 2000s, purchasing agents from all over the world descended on China to buy manufactured goods. Each year they bought more and more. And almost all of them were driven to China by what was to become standard currency in the language of corporate purchasing executives: "the China price."

China had emerged as the lowest-cost place on earth to buy goods of all kinds. Walmart was transformed into an American store jammed with Chinese stuff, seemingly overnight. The China price was driven by Chinese culture. The Chinese people watch the money. Even the money for paper cups—as the following story illustrates.

After attending a conference at First Auto Works, a group of foreign executives were seated in a van, ready to return to their hotels. A young Chinese woman came running out of an office building, looking panic-stricken. She was bundled up in several layers, as is common in Northeast China in winter, and she clutched a small piece of paper.

One of the executives inside the van tapped the Chinese driver on the shoulder and signaled for him to stay put. They recognized this woman, heading their way. She was one of the aces on the team that organized the special seminar on automotive design engineering. As she got closer to the van, they could see that her brow was furrowed and her lips were taut and trembling. Something was obviously wrong.

The driver opened the front doors to the van and, with an air of tired indifference, as if he had seen this kind of thing before, yelled, "What is it?"

"It's the cups!"

"It's the what?" the driver shouted back over the din of his engine.

"The cups. They paid for the extra bottles of Coca-Cola this afternoon. But who's going to pay for the extra paper cups?"

With that, she handed over a slightly crumpled sheet of paper with some Chinese characters and a number on it.

It was a bill for the extra paper cups, totaling 26 renminbi—just over US$3 at the time. One of the Europeans had ordered more paper cups for their meeting. That created a problem: the cups had to be paid for. And now the Europeans were leaving, and that would mean someone from the Chinese company would be forced to pay for the paper cups. But no one had money—at least, no one had money to pay for the Europeans' cups.

The Europeans looked at one another in quiet astonishment. The woman stood in the cold at the base of the van steps and gazed, unblinking, at the visitors.

"Well, OK, then," said the leader of the delegation. He dug into his pocket, pulled out three 10-RMB notes, and handed them over to her. She took the money, did an about-face, and hurried back to the building, as though concerned that the visitors might change their minds.

This is the norm in China. Chinese people are very careful with accounts. They watch the money. Someone has to pay for things, and the Chinese always prefer that someone to be someone else.

"Keep the change," an expression so familiar to Americans, would sound naïve or idiotic (or both) to the average Chinese. To them, money is still a scarce resource. You don't just let someone keep the change.

This obsession with money may seem odd to people in America, who see headlines about China's 875,000 millionaires and, according to a 2010 tally, more than 100 billionaires. There is no denying that some Chinese have amassed stunning amounts of wealth. But 875,000 people out of 1.4 billion is less than 0.10 percent.

To get a feel for how tiny 0.01 percent is, imagine going to Michigan's football stadium on a Saturday afternoon, with its capacity to seat 104,000 people. Around 103,950 spectators would arrive on bicycle or on foot. A few dozen would drive up in Chevys or Hyundais. Sifting through all that mass of humanity, however, you would find just a single individual wealthy enough to own a luxury car like a Mercedes-Benz.

If you continue to think of China's population as a crowd of sports spectators, the vast majority of fans will be rushing to their seats, concerned that someone else may take their place before they get there. Yes, they have a ticket. But when there are a lot of people and a limited number of seats, it is better to claim your seat early, just in case. Who knows, maybe someone else will show up with a ticket for your seat, too. Then what? Turn to one of the "mysterious deciders" for a resolution?

The cause of this angst is crowding and uncertainty. China's land mass is about the same as the United States, but most of China's population is situated along or near the east coast. And there are almost five Chinese citizens for every American. Imagine the entire U.S. population living in the States east of the Mississippi. Then multiply America's population by five. Things would get very crowded very quickly. That is how the world looks to most of the Chinese people every day. So they are very careful—many would say tight-fisted—with money.

There is a vibrant and fast-expanding middle class in China. But do not confuse Chinese middle class with American middle class. Take the example of Ms. Liu, a nanny working in Shanghai. Her salary, at $320 per month, is more than double the national average. But she still has to watch every dime. There is no central heating in Shanghai, even though temperatures fall into the high 30s during the winter. When asked what she does about the cold weather, Liu says, "Oh, who can afford a heater? Look, my husband and I take home about $400 a month. Our daughter's tuition alone next year is $3,500. Then there is rent. And food. What if we get sick? That's getting really terrifying. You think we have money left over for heating? No, no, no. I just wear more layers."

America's automakers—the Big Three—were once careful with their funds, too. There was a time when a worker's wages at General Motors, Chrysler, and Ford were directly correlated to the value of his or her inputs. The government set a minimum wage, to be sure. Every dollar above and beyond that wage, however, was an investment calculated to earn a return for the company. That was before the unions gained power and gathered so much strength. Over time, the unions grew so dominant that workers' wages were tied not to his or her contributions to the company's bottom line, but to arbitrary metrics like the number of years on the job.

Since 1980 China has been moving away from the concept of an "iron rice bowl" society (China's socialist system that guaranteed jobs for life during the 1960s and 1970s), while the Detroit automakers and the United Auto Workers union were traveling, inexorably, ever closer to such a system. China was moving toward capitalism while Detroit was moving toward socialism. The differences in direction became patently clear when it came time to set workers' wages at Shanghai General Motors.

For management at Shanghai GM, the question was straightforward: What would be the right amount of money to attract capable workers, while not overpaying?

Employers in Shanghai pay into two buckets. One is a monthly wage. The other is the "Si Jing" (four economic) funds mandated by the Shanghai City government. Payments into the "Si Jing" cover an individual's pension, housing, medical coverage, and unemployment. These payments make Shanghai one of the most expensive places in China to employ people today. As of 2010, Shanghai paid the highest minimum wage in China, with a rate of $164 per month, according to the Ministry of Human Resources and Social Security. Wages at foreign joint ventures like Shanghai GM were well above the minimum wage set by the State. But they were still less than $5 per hour.

In recent years, many manufacturing companies have left Shanghai for more affordable locations in central and western China. Jiangxi and Anhui, two provinces within a day's drive of Shanghai, have much lower minimum wages—$105 per month, according to JP Morgan Chase. But in the early 2000s, Shanghai manufacturing labor was still competitive within China. And compared with labor in the United States, the wages in Shanghai could have been on some other planet.

In the early 2000s, wages and benefits for workers at plants controlled by the United Auto Workers in Detroit amounted to $70 per hour. In Shanghai, the minimum wage for factory workers was $1 per hour. To put this in perspective, you could hire seventy Chinese workers for every one American UAW laborer. And in China there were another one hundred workers eager to take their place in the event of injury, fatigue, or any other misfortune that might knock a Chinese out of his or her job.

It's easy to see why American car companies no longer build affordable, small cars. Wages—coupled with extensive and expensive benefits—are simply too high to allow manufacturers to make a small car and break even. It would be like the young child manning his summertime lemonade stand taking a union-mandated salary of $25 per hour. He'd never sell enough glasses of 10-cent lemonade to pay himself that salary, let alone for the ingredients from his mom. He might think about raising prices for the lemonade. But then no one would stop to buy a glass.

China seemed to offer a way forward. But a couple of things stood in the way of producing small cars with SAIC. First, while the Chinese were getting better at assembling vehicles, they were still very weak in the critical steps involved in developing a car—the design, engineering, and manufacturing processes. "We had a couple hundred Chinese engineers on staff, but only one guy with a driver's license," was the inside joke shared by American employees working at Shanghai GM.

A second and even more significant downside to making cars in China was the money. If GM jointly developed a car with SAIC, then half of all revenues and profits from that car would go directly into Chinese pockets. The "source profits"—money made by selling parts from GM in Europe or North America to the joint venture, Shanghai GM—would evaporate.

Equally troubling, GM would no longer enjoy sole claim to the intellectual property for new products. GM and SAIC could both claim ownership of the product. That meant, technically, that the Shanghai GM joint venture could build cars in China and ship them to any market in the world, without prior approval from GM.

Rudy Schlais, now president of GM Asia Pacific, looked for other options in the region. Japan was a dead end. Since the 1980s, GM had been partnering with Suzuki and Isuzu and Subaru in the hopes of learning how to make small cars. But GM's will to learn was weak, and the Japanese were not much inclined to openly share their secrets for manufacturing at low cost. Even when GM tied up a successful joint venture with Toyota in California, the new learning stayed at the plant or got buried in GM's massive bureaucracy. Thailand presented an option, too. GM had built a massive new plant there just prior to the Asian financial crisis in 1997. Local demand for cars had dropped by more than half. So there was plenty of spare capacity to make cars in the modern plant located on the eastern seaboard near Bangkok. But the Thais were only a few years ahead of the Chinese when it came to the art and technical skills required to develop cars.

The only real remedy for GM's glaring weakness in small, competitive cars was found in Korea. The Asian financial crisis had dealt a punishing blow not only to Thailand and its neighbors but also to automakers in Korea.

Kia was on the brink of bankruptcy when the government instructed Hyundai to absorb its closest competitor, forming the giant conglomerate we know today as Hyundai-Kia. Daewoo, a company that had earlier married General Motors in a 50–50 partnership only to divorce in the early 1990s, enjoyed no such government-mandated lifeline. The company went bankrupt in 2000 under the weight of an estimated $17 billion in debts.

Schlais saw an opportunity. In a 2011 email message, Schlais recalled the number one reason for the acquisition:

> Daewoo had done an excellent job on developing new projects using a Global Project Approach—define what was needed in the product and then use globally available resources to accomplish the task vs. many others including GM which used only internal resources.

In other words, Daewoo was willing to find ways to work with other GM fiefdoms. Schlais believed that acquiring Daewoo would give GM access to the seemingly impenetrable Korean car market. But the main advantage in purchasing Daewoo would be in securing access to people who worked at cost levels that would at last allow GM to build small cars profitably.

In a very complex acquisition, GM secured control of Daewoo's best assets for $400 million in cash. In hindsight, the purchase price was remarkably low. GM had purchased an entire car company for only slightly more than its initial investment in the Shanghai GM joint venture.

The new company was named the GM Daewoo Automotive Technology Company, GM DAT for short. General Motors was not the sole investor, however. Joining the purchase were the Korean Development Bank and, a couple of months later, Suzuki Motor. GM's initial 67-percent ownership stake gave it effective control over all facets of the operation. The Korean Development Bank (KDB) was there to contribute financing. Suzuki was on hand to lend know-how in small cars as GM DAT got back on its feet.

But the minority ownership list did not stop with KDB and Suzuki. Also holding shares in GM's new subsidiary in Korea was the Shanghai Auto Industry Corporation. GM had invited SAIC into the deal because it anticipated an important role for Korea in the China business: Korea would, in the future, be the key source of products assembled by Shanghai GM in China. GM's vision was to design and engineer smaller cars in Korea for the Korean market, for export markets worldwide and also for assembly at the Shanghai GM plants in China.

SAIC would have an incentive to help make GM DAT a success because the Korean firm would be the supplier of future products and because SAIC, as a shareholder, could earn profits from the Korean operation too. The move also gave added weight to GM's widely-advertised notion that GM and SAIC were in a very close partnership, one that knew no borders.

It was not all upside in Korea, though. There were some substantial risks. First, the Hyundai-Kia tie-up meant that GM DAT would be forced to do battle with an awesome competitor inside Korea, one that controlled 90 percent of the Korean market. Second, GM's earlier joint venture with Daewoo had failed in no small part because of misunderstandings and miscommunications between the Koreans and the Americans. So there were no positive precedents to point to.

Most worrisome, though, was the aggressive nature of the Korean unions. The automotive workers unions in Korea are among the most militant in the world. In fact, on the day the GM-Daewoo deal was signed, several dozen union workers showed up at the hotel where the event was scheduled to take place. A threatened sit-in by union workers forced everyone to shuttle, impromptu, to the Korean Development Bank to finalize the handshakes and signatures. Schlais later recalled that "the deal was very favorable, but with a high risk. [That is] one of the reasons Suzuki and SAIC were asked to participate with GM."

The GM DAT ownership structure would become a flashpoint of controversy in 2009 when GM experienced financial meltdowns.

In going with Korea as a strategic solution, GM was making a big bet that it could keep the workers content enough not to strike for higher wages. Korean living standards were much, much higher than those in China and Southeast Asia, and wages were much higher too. It was an open question as to how long Korea could remain a viable site for low-cost vehicle production. Schlais recalls the sentiment at the time: Obviously many worries and concerns, but "no pain—no gain."

When the deal was completed in April 2002, there was a collective sigh of relief. Finally, it seemed, General Motors could hope to build small cars at competitive prices.

While GM was negotiating the deal in Korea, Phil Murtaugh had made an important move inside China. He made a recommendation to Chen Hong, president of Shanghai GM: hire Joseph Liu to take charge of sales and marketing. Up to that point, Liu had served as CEO of General Motors in Taiwan. Murtaugh had been promoted to chairman and CEO of GM China in 2000, but in making the recommendation, he remained totally engaged in the operations at Shanghai GM.

Liu arrived in the middle of 2001 and was soon tasked with a formidable job. As Liu later recalled, GM chairman Jack Smith paid him a visit and said, "Joseph, our plant here is designed to make a hundred thousand cars a year, so please do whatever you can to get us there." Shanghai GM would sell just fifty-eight thousand units in 2001, its third year of operation. Liu also needed the Korean acquisition to work.

David Chen was now GM China's executive director of planning and new business development. Murtaugh sent him to Korea at the end of 2001 to assess which Daewoo products would be most suitable for China. Chen quickly identified one small, one medium, and one large car as potential future products—cars to be built in China as early as the summer of 2003.

The GM executives felt good about the fact that the Koreans seemed almost as careful about money as the Chinese. After the bankruptcy, the Korean management and workers were being given a second chance. They knew there might not be a third one. With little more than a sliver of the Korean domestic market, Daewoo workers understood that, to keep their jobs, they would have to export. And to export with sustained success meant setting and meeting world-class standards for cost and quality.

In his prepared remarks on the day of the acquisition, Jack Smith spoke to the strategic importance of the deal: "This is a great opportunity working with Daewoo and with our research and development, which we can bring here to take advantage of what Daewoo does very well, which is to develop new products in a very fast manner."

Indeed, GM needed new products in a "very fast manner," especially in China. The Buick Sail was Shanghai GM's lone small-car offering. And although demand for the Sail was in line with planning, the product was but a temporary fix. The Sail achieved sales of 26,500 units in 2001, enough for the dealers to start to feel better about their investments.

Up to this point, the Sail was operating in an environment of limited competition. But that was about to change in a big way. Toyota, Nissan, Hyundai, and Ford were signing joint ventures to build cars in China, starting later in 2002.

China had formally joined the World Trade Organization at the end of 2001, which opened the floodgates to new competition. As part of its accession to the WTO, China agreed to drop its long-standing cap on which foreign car companies could invest and what automobiles could be manufactured. Chinese car buyers did not know it at the time, but the car market offerings were about to go from desert-dry to tropically luxuriant. In 2000, Chinese consumers had fewer than ten different cars to choose from. By 2011, that number of choices would skyrocket to more than 275.

Ford's arrival did not scare GM. But the Asian manufacturers' did. Toyota, Nissan, and Hyundai excelled at reliable and afford-able small cars. Car loans were still in their infancy in China, accounting for less than 5 percent of transactions. So a new car purchase would almost always be made in cash—cash saved care-fully over many years of work—plus cash borrowed from family and friends.

The Japanese automakers, in particular, were well-acquainted with money-careful Asian buyers. They had been building and selling cars to the same kinds of people in East Asia and Southeast Asia since the 1970s. GM and Ford had earlier left those same Asian markets because they were unable to build cars at affordable prices. Or, for that matter, cars with steering wheels on the right-hand side.

GM desperately needed to tap into the Korean strength in devel-oping cars in a very fast manner, as Chairman Smith had said. But Smith and his team of GM executives in Asia could never have imagined just how quickly Daewoo products would enter the China market. Nor could they have imagined the utterly unexpected way in which Daewoo cars would soon appear in China.

General Motors in China
Key Development Milestones (1992–2011)

July, 1992	SAIC first contacts GM about cooperation
March 25, 1997	GM and SAIC sign JV agreement to create Shanghai General Motors
December 17, 1998	First Buick Century produced at Shanghai GM
June 4, 2002	SAIC-GM-Wuling joint venture formed
December 2004	Shanghai GM achieves highest sales among China joint ventures
March 31, 2005	Phil Murtaugh resigns, Kevin Wale takes over in May
January 5, 2006	Shanghai GM produces its 1 millionth vehicle
February 22, 2008	Shanghai GM produces its 2 millionth vehicle
December 4, 2009	GM announces one percent equity sale to SAIC, reducing GM's share to 49%
January 11, 2010	Launch of Chevrolet New Sail, Shanghai GM's first jointly owned car
2010	GM and Chinese partners sell 2.3 million vehicles in China, topping sales in the US
January, 2011	Shanghai GM introduces the Chevrolet Volt electric vehicle

Sources: *General Motors China and Dunne & Company Ltd.*

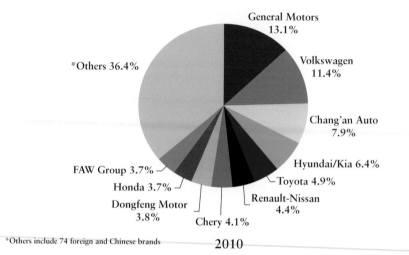

China's Top 10
Light Vehicle Market Shares

General Motors
13.1%

Volkswagen
11.4%

*Others 36.4%

Chang'an Auto
7.9%

Hyundai/Kia 6.4%

FAW Group 3.7%

Toyota 4.9%

Honda 3.7%

Renault-Nissan
4.4%

Dongfeng Motor
3.8%

Chery 4.1%

*Others include 74 foreign and Chinese brands

2010

Sources: J.P. Morgan, GM China, Dunne & Company

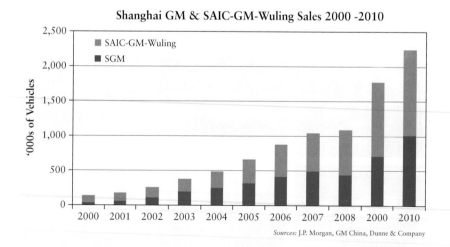

Shanghai GM & SAIC-GM-Wuling Sales 2000 -2010

■ SAIC-GM-Wuling
■ SGM

'000s of Vehicles

2,500
2,000
1,500
1,000
500
0

2000 2001 2002 2003 2004 2005 2006 2007 2008 2000 2010

Sources: J.P. Morgan, GM China, Dunne & Company

The Many Detroits of China
Top 10 Passenger Vehicle Makers

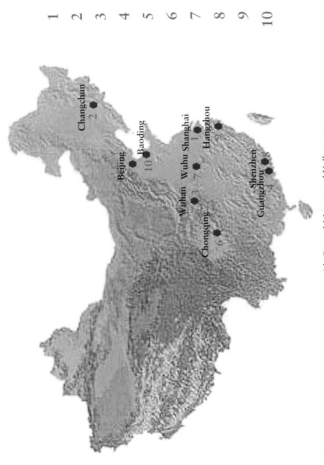

1		Shanghai Auto
2		First Auto
3		Dongfeng Motors
4		ChangAn
5		Beijing Auto
6		Guangzhou Auto
7		Chery
8		BYD
9		Geely
10		Great Wall

Shanghai Auto runs separate joint ventures with General Motors and Volkswagen

Shanghai's taxi fleet is dominated by the antiquated VW Santana 2000—thanks to special political and commercial arrangements. The 2000 is an updated version of the original VW Santana model that began production in China in 1985. There were an estimated 1.7 million Santana and Santana 2000 models running on Chinese roads in 2011.

The first Buick Century (*Xin Shiji* in Chinese) rolled off the assembly line in December 1998 at Shanghai GM's brand new factory in Pudong. Soon after its initial launch the Century confronted unexpected competition from the VW Passat and the Honda Accord. The 3-liter engine Century was known among Chinese buyers for being prestigious, safe—and gas guzzling.

Chery's QQ (bottom), a near perfect replica of the Chevrolet Spark, was the first to go on sale in China in 2003. That the QQ, a copy model, could be launched into the market *before* the original Chevrolet Spark was a source of great surprise and frustration to leaders at Shanghai GM. The QQ outsold the Spark by a ratio of 5 to 1 thanks to its much cheaper price. GM sued in Chinese and Korean courts for infringement of intellectual property, but to no avail.

Philip Murtaugh was Executive Vice-President of Shanghai GM from 1997 to 1999 and Chairman and CEO of General Motors China from 2000 to 2005. Under his direction Shanghai GM developed from a start-up into a $6 billion dollar company and one of GM's most profitable operations worldwide.

Shanghai GM's big gamble in 2003 to source products from Korea and badge them as Buicks and Chevrolets paid off handsomely. The Buick Excelle is a perennial top-seller in the China market, appealing to middle class, urban professionals and young families. Most of the Buicks and Chevrolets sold in China in 2010 were developed in GM's Korean subsidiary, GM Korea.

Kevin Wale (fourth from left), president of GM China, joins staff members in a cake cutting ceremony to mark production of the two millionth vehicle at Shanghai GM. It took GM eight years to build its one millionth vehicle. Just two years later, in 2008, Shanghai GM built its two millionth.

Demand for the Shanghai GM Wuling Sunshine exploded in China's 3rd and 4th tier cities, with sales topping one million in 2010. An affordable price, reliability and functionality were its key selling points. Murtaugh and Hu pushed for investment into Wuling in 2002 despite strong objections from GM headquarters in Detroit.

Chevrolet's New Sail marked a watershed in product development at Shanghai GM. It was the joint venture's first model starting under $9,000. Intellectual property of the New Sail belonged to Shanghai GM, not exclusively to GM. And the product set export records of more than 10,000 cars in its first year.

Cars of every brand and model jousting for space on a Shanghai street. As the world's largest car market—11 million passenger vehicles sold in 2010—Chinese car drivers' demand for oil has soared. Planners in Beijing are working hard to steer the industry towards alternative energies, especially electric vehicles.

14

THE CHERY SURPRISE

Long before GM acquired Daewoo in 2002, Yin Tongyao had already settled on a name for his new venture. Yin Tongyao is president and founder of Chery Automobile, a state enterprise located in the small city of Wuhu in the hard-luck, landlocked province of Anhui.

Seated in his colorless, Spartan office—the kind often seen in Chinese state enterprises—Mr. Yin, clad in a short-sleeved, open-collared oxford shirt, explained, "I wanted something optimistic, bright—but also something that people would remember. I searched words in the English dictionary. I found *cheerful*, and I liked it. So I thought about 'Cheery.' But then, to make the name stick in people's minds, I took out an 'e.' Then it became Chery." Mr. Yin grinned a little in pride at his own invention. "That's how the company got the name Chery."

Today Chery is one of China's leading carmakers, with more than two million autos on the road.

In 2003 Chery—the cheerful company—stunned General Motors with a not-so-cheery surprise. Six years after its formation, the company had masterminded and executed a very clever coup.

The company had come into existence quietly in 1997 as an engine maker. In time, Chery secured rights to build cars despite strong opposition by central government planners in Beijing. Officials in charge of the automotive industry gave car production licenses only to companies featured in the central government's official plans. Chery was never part of the official plan.

Yet by 2000, through perseverance, luck, and deft political maneuvering, Chery had evolved from an engine maker to a producer of small, affordable cars. Chery initially assembled cars that resembled an old model built by SEAT, a Spanish subsidiary of Volkswagen.

That's how things can go in China. It may begin with a discussion like this:

Central Government:	You are forbidden from building cars. Don't even think about it.
Wuhu Secretary General:	No cars? Okay, but is it all right to build engines?
Central Government Official:	Yes, engines are permitted.
Wuhu Secretary General:	Okay, I will build engines.

Then a year later, the conversation starts anew:

Wuhu Secretary General:	Look, I cannot find any buyers for my engines. Can I build cars to put them in?
Central Government Official:	Absolutely not. We told you already last year!
Wuhu Secretary General:	But the people in our city need jobs. It is not fair that Shanghai can give its people jobs and we cannot. How about if we build cars but promise to sell them only in our city?
Central Government:	To be sold *only in your city*?
Wuhu Secretary General:	Yes, only here in Wuhu.
Central Government:	Okay, but not a single sale beyond your city limits!
Wuhu Secretary General:	Yes, of course. We will strictly control the sales.

At the turn of the century, Chery had all the appearance of a harmless state enterprise located in a remote town. Few people in the industry had ever heard of the company, and fewer still had heard the name of its leader, Yin Tongyao. Yet, just two years later, Chery had gained the ability to make a small car that would take GM by complete surprise. But how?

It is not every manager of a state enterprise that gets to name his company. In fact, most state-owned companies are given pre-dictable, neutral names like First Auto Works (because it was China's first major vehicle producer after the revolution in 1949) or Beijing Automotive (because the company belongs to the city of Beijing). Then again, most people who run state enterprises are not as talented, inventive, and hard-working as Yin Tongyao.

Yin is a native of Anhui. As many residents of south central Chinese provinces tend to do, he left home after graduation and took a job in a more developed part of the country. He was assigned a job at the central government–owned First Auto Works (which later became First Automotive Works–Volkswagen). That was the custom for Chinese college graduates during the 1980s and early 1990s. When you finished your degree, the state determined where you should go to work.

In Yin's case, the destination was the snowy city of Changchun, more than a thousand miles away. Situated at about the same latitude as the state of Maine, Changchun is bitter cold in the winter.

But Yin's assignment to FAW was a good thing for him. Many of the nation's best and brightest engineers were sent to Changchun to help the country build trucks and buses—vehicles that served the people. Only a few years after Yin arrived, he caught his first break. The leadership at FAW decided that it was time to move beyond trucks and buses and into the business of producing cars.

At the time, FAW was making only a few hundred bulky "Red Flag" sedans each year for senior party officials. The always-black Red Flag was based on the 1955 Chrysler Imperial C69. There was little prestige and even less money in making old-fashioned cars for the Party leaders. In 1991, FAW negotiated a new joint venture with Volkswagen AG, FAW-VW, to build VW and Audi cars.

Under the terms of the deal, Volkswagen would contribute the plant and equipment and FAW would provide the land. VW had no intention of building a brand-new plant in China. Instead, it proposed that an existing VW plant in Westmoreland, Pennsylvania, would be dismantled and shipped to China. Yin, then in his late twenties, was assigned to a team of Chinese from FAW to travel to Pennsylvania and spend weeks overseeing the transfer of the plant by ship back to Changchun.

It is no simple task to tear down, move, and rebuild a car plant. There is plenty that can go wrong. Yin recalled the need to carefully document every piece of the plant and equipment so that they could be reassembled with the least amount of difficulty once they arrived in China. It was painstaking work. But by doing the teardown, Yin learned a big lesson, one that he would apply in the future. He saw, first-hand, that it was possible to break a massive car plant down into tiny bits and then reconstruct it from the ground up on the other side of the planet.

Back at FAW, Yin rose quickly through the ranks and was soon promoted to the vital position of assembly plant manager at the FAW-VW joint venture. There he supervised the coming together of all parts into a final product. He saw how the chassis, the engine, the transmission, the instrumental panel, the seats, and the body panels all came together to produce a final car. The process became ingrained in his brain, in much the same way that a kid memorizes a Lego set by putting it together over and over again.

In the summer of 1996, Yin took his company vacation time to travel home to Anhui. It was during this trip that he met Zhan Xialai, the Party Secretary General of Wuhu, a driven character who had a vision for his town.

"We're going to build a car company here," Zhan informed Yin. "I'll take care of the money and the politics. I need a guy to build the cars, and I understand that you are exactly the right man for the job."

The idea of building cars in Wuhu was crazy. The city was remote; even worse, it had no industrial infrastructure. The predominantly agrarian labor force had no experience in building cars. Incomes were among the lowest in the country, as low as $300 per year on average. It would be hard to select a less suitable place to launch a new car company.

Then there were the policy constraints. Everyone knew that the central government kept a stranglehold on licenses to produce cars. There was no way Wuhu would get an okay from Beijing to make cars.

Zhan reassured Yin: "You let me take care of the licenses; you just focus on getting some cars built here."

The secretary general was just persuasive enough to convince Yin to resign from his prestigious job at FAW-VW and take on this new challenge back home, however outlandish it seemed at the time. Yin shortly began looking around for ways to build a car. But where to start? The Secretary General had already won the central government officials over to the idea of allowing Wuhu to build engines, if not cars.

So Yin traveled to Europe in search of an engine. He discovered an old Ford engine plant for sale in the United Kingdom. Just as he had done in Westmoreland, he bought the engine line, had it dismantled, and rebuilt the line in Wuhu. Just like that, the young company was in the business of making engines. But like the ill-fated BeiNei plant in Beijing, Yin's engine plant had no customers. Who would want to buy an old Ford engine?

Meanwhile, the Secretary General's efforts to win approval for car production were meeting strong resistance in Beijing. The central government officials were adamant about not letting the car-making doors open, lest every other small town in China start applying for the rights to make cars too. Such a scenario would create a fine mess, they warned. China's mission was to consolidate the industry around a few leading companies, like Shanghai Automotive, Beijing Automotive, and FAW. To them, the idea of building cars in Wuhu was a joke.

But the Secretary General did not think it was a joke. In fact, he was determined to find a way to push things along. There is a Chinese saying: "Take the indirect way and make it the direct way." This is what the mayor did.

Through very senior contacts in the Party, the Secretary General suggested and got approval for an investment in Wuhu. Not any old investment. An investment by SAIC—in Chery Automobile!

SAIC, it should be pointed out, initially wanted no part of the investment. It was quite content to build its businesses with GM and VW. But a directive from the highest levels of power in Beijing essentially forced the hand of SAIC. Chery's "godfather" in Beijing trumped SAIC's "godfather" in Beijing. There was nothing to discuss.

Somebody was owed a favor, and it was payback time.

SAIC reluctantly became a 20-percent shareholder in Chery. The Secretary General then made a fresh appeal to the central government: "Look, now that Chery is part of the SAIC Group, and SAIC qualifies to build cars, should Chery not qualify for a license to build cars, too?"

Despite the sour taste in their mouths, the central government officials could no longer refuse. Before long, just as the Secretary General had promised, Yin found himself with a green light to build cars.

News of the investment would not be published in a newspaper or made public in any form. It was a "*neibu*" or an internal issue. It is unclear whether SAIC mentioned this new shareholding in Chery to its partners, GM and Volkswagen. They may have reasoned that it made no sense to alarm foreigners about a family affair strictly between Chinese state enterprises and the government.

At the time, the SAIC leaders considered Chery a minor nuisance that would go away before long. But Chery had no intention of going away. On the contrary, the little company from Wuhu was just getting started down a path that would ultimately cause SAIC no end of consternation.

Yin had an engine. But getting an entire car assembled would be more difficult. He would need not only a car prototype and an assembly line, but also all of the parts that go into a car—the transmission, the steering system, the brakes, the body panels, the electronics, and so on. Yin got his break in Spain, where he happened upon a shuttered car assembly plant that belonged to SEAT. The last car produced in the SEAT plant happened to be the same basic car as the Volkswagen Jetta, which was being produced at the FAW-VW plant in Changchun—the same plant where Yin was director of final assembly. What a stroke of good luck!

By acquiring the SEAT car assembly plant, Yin understood that he could secure all the parts he needed right inside China simply by going to the parts makers that were already supplying the Volkswagen Jetta. It was almost too good to be true. Yet true it was.

The parts manufacturers were a little edgy about supplying the same parts to Chery that they sold to FAW-VW for the Jetta. But at the same time, the extra orders went directly to their bottom line. They would take the business and explain to Volkswagen later, if necessary.

In early 1999, cars with the Chery brand name began to appear on Chinese roads. They were called the Chery Fengyun (Wind and Clouds). The Chery's front grille and taillights looked different enough from those of the Volkswagen Jetta. But the guts of the two cars, aside from Chery's Ford engine, were virtually identical. Yin had created a SEAT clone in China—a very close cousin to the Jetta.

Chinese customers could buy a new Chery for just over $10,000, far below the Jetta price of $15,500. Yin and Chery were able to offer such aggressive prices because they had incurred almost no research and development costs. A new car typically requires a billion dollars or more to design and engineer. But Chery was simply taking an existing design and parts and cobbling them together into a new car.

Before long, despite those initial promises to keep the Chery local, its sales extended beyond the Wuhu city limits. "How can we deny any Chinese person the right to buy a Chery with his hard-earned money?" was the rhetorical question sent by Wuhu to the authorities in Beijing.

No right-minded bureaucrat in the capital with any ambitions for advancing his career wanted to take on that question. And so the Chery cars began to surface throughout the country, from Beijing in the North to Guangzhou in the South to the inland markets like Chengdu, Anhui, and Changsha, where shoppers were the most price-sensitive.

At Volkswagen headquarters and inside China, the Germans were understandably vexed when they saw the Jetta cousin first appear on the streets of Shanghai and Beiing. But they were also slow to react. Volkswagen may have been under the influence of that powerful, hard-to-resist drug called hubris. Who could blame them? Volkswagen's joint ventures in China controlled 50 percent of the market in China and profits kept getting bigger, year after year. Chery was a nothing company from a nothing town, a state enterprise with no genuine expertise in developing cars. The prevailing thought within VW was that Chery would soon collapse under the weight of its own ineptitude and poor quality.

The Germans were not completely wrong about the quality. Because the Chery Fengyun had been essentially cobbled together from many disparate locations (a British engine, a Spanish assembly plant, and parts made in China), it was difficult to assemble the car in a consistent and reliable manner. Chery cars soon developed a reputation as cheap to buy, but requiring regular visits to the repair shop.

On the Internet and in the newspapers, people quickly adopted a derisive slogan: "*Qirui, Qirui, xiu che pai dui*," which translated to "Chery, Chery, get in line for repairing." Whereas the Japanese and Korean consumers will rally around their homegrown cars, the Chinese will do so if, and only if, they are good value for money. The Chinese priority is generally pocketbook first and Chinese nationalism second. If Chery was prone to quality problems, the average Chinese customer would have no qualms about spurning it.

It was clear that in order to achieve the mayor's vision for a great car company in Wuhu, Chery quality would have to improve. The next product would be key. Yin had used his experience to craft a car without any real research and development work. The results, measured in sales, were better than expected for a start-up company. But Yin knew that tactics used to bring the first car together would get him only so far. He needed a fresh approach. But what might that be?

Phil Murtaugh and his team at Shanghai GM would have heard about Chery and the copycat of the Jetta. But Volkswagen's small drama would not have been high on their list of worries. Instead, Shanghai GM focused on bringing new products to market—affordable small cars made at GM's new subsidiary in Korea. Even before the acquisition of Daewoo was complete, Shanghai GM had already identified the first two products it would like to bring to China.

One car would be a small four-door sedan geared for urban professionals and their families—a car originally called the Daewoo Lacetti. A roomy, if ordinary-looking commuter car that got good gas mileage, it would be priced between $15,000 and $20,000. It would be called the Buick Excelle.

The other was a cute-looking micro car called the Daewoo Matiz, styled by the respected Italian design house Ital Design. This car would be priced under $10,000 and was aimed directly at the expected giant wave of first-time buyers on tight budgets. The tiny Matiz, designed in Italy for a Korean company acquired by General Motors, would be christened the Chevrolet Spark when it was reincarnated for the China market.

For Shanghai GM, timing was critical. With China's entry into the WTO, the young joint venture would soon be knocking heads in China with the toughest competitors from around the world. Toyota was coming. So were Hyundai, Nissan, and Ford. Ambitious production timelines were set. The Excelle would be launched in the middle of 2003, and the Spark would follow a few months later. The race to get the new products to market was on.

Back at Chery, Yin was pursuing his own kind of race. He is the kind of quiet engineer who, confident in his talents, is at ease with himself. He is not concerned about what others think. When a group of five senior executives from an American company paid a visit to his hotel during an auto show in Beijing, Yin invited them up to his room instead of coming to see them in the lobby coffee shop. Greeting the guests in his socks, his hair slightly askew from a late-afternoon nap, Yin directed the Americans to sit on a small sofa inside his hotel room. Then he poured tea into tiny cups for them. It is this unassuming and serene manner that often led competitors to underestimate him.

Shanghai GM executives cannot be faulted for underestimating Yin. They had hardly heard of him and would not recognize him if they saw him walking down the street. Their top priority was bringing the Buick Excelle and the Chevrolet Spark to market.

A big part of the effort in launching a car is for the purchasing department to sign contracts with scores of parts makers for each vehicle. Purchasing executives from Shanghai GM first heard about Chery's new product from its own suppliers. When Shanghai GM approached parts makers to supply the necessary components for the Spark, they were told that many of the companies had already signed contracts with Chery to supply identical parts! *But that's impossible,* they thought. There was no way that Chery could be building the Chevrolet Spark. The Chevrolet Spark had never appeared in public, and production would not begin until the end of 2003! How could a Chinese company copy a car yet to be built? It made no sense.

Chery was indeed well on track to launch its own new car, called the Chery QQ. The Chery QQ and the Chevrolet Spark looked like identical twins. Shanghai GM engineers would later buy a Chery QQ, bring it to the factory, tear it down piece by piece, and set each part side by side with the Spark's. The engineering specifications or "mathematics" were identical. Chery was building the same little Korean product that GM was planning to launch!

When the Chery QQ made its first public appearance at the Shanghai Auto Show in the spring of 2003, public relations people were unabashed in their enthusiasm for the new car. "We want to make the coolest car on the planet," they said. In July, they launched the car at a price of just under $8,000. Shanghai GM would not introduce the Chevrolet Spark until December, six months after the Chery QQ. And the Spark's price would be 20 percent higher than that of the QQ.

GM people were understandably confused: How in the world had Chery managed to copy a car before its launch? Not a rough copy—an identical twin. There was only one explanation: somewhere, somehow, Chery had secured access to the original drawings and engineering details for the car. They were not only working from the same set of plans as Shanghai GM, but they were doing it faster. Six months faster.

When GM turned to its partner, SAIC, for advice, they were handed another unpleasant surprise: SAIC was a 20-percent shareholder in Chery! SAIC was red-faced about the affair and explained how the central government had forced it to be an unwilling investor in Chery from the beginning.

It had no role in Chery's acquisition of the drawings, senior executives from SAIC explained. At GM's urging, SAIC soon sold its shares in Chery. The Chery "godfather" in the central government acquiesced to SAIC's divestment in part because Chery had already achieved its goal by becoming a carmaker on its own.

GM was stinging. According to suppliers, Murtaugh held a "come to Jesus" meeting at which he issued a warning to parts companies: "If you supply the Chery QQ, you will have no more business with Shanghai GM." The suppliers had no doubt that Murtaugh was serious. But what could they do at this juncture, having already purchased the equipment and signed contracts with Chery? To get out of the pickle with Shanghai GM, many declared that they were supplying components for "Chery's other products and not the QQ." But reality was a different story.

Next, GM lawyers took up the case. They brought a complaint to court in China not once, but twice. On both occasions, GM lawyers showed photos of the two vehicles. To any man on the street, it was obvious that the two cars were the same. There was no argument there. But the key to the case was proving that Chery had wrongfully secured the drawings. Both times, the court ruled that GM did not provide sufficient evidence to show that Chery had stolen intellectual property from them. GM attempted one more lawsuit, this time in Korea. But the result was inconclusive. Ultimately, GM and Shanghai GM had no choice but to put the matter behind them.

How Chery actually acquired the original drawings for the Chevy Spark has never been publicly confirmed. Anecdotal evidence suggests a scenario like this: While Daewoo Motors was in court receivership in 2001, an agent from Taiwan brokered a secret agreement whereby senior engineers from Daewoo would channel the drawings to Taiwan and then on to Wuhu for an undisclosed fee. Because Daewoo was in bankruptcy, it was possible the Daewoo engineers felt that the company was doomed and would never resume production. To them, it may have seemed like an opportunity to get something in return for their hard work in designing and developing a smart-looking small car.

From Chery's perspective, there was no problem with the QQ. The company had paid for the drawings at a time when Daewoo was in bankruptcy. GM was not yet the owner, so Chery was not taking anything from them. According to some sources, Chery had even sent a letter to GM asking for the rights to produce the QQ under license. But GM rejected the request. GM's lawyers, while negotiating the purchase of Daewoo, probably never thought to include a provision that would cover an event such as the leaking of future product drawings to a little-known Chinese company called Chery!

It takes great courage to hold one's ground and press forward when the walls around you seem to be crumbling. At this juncture, Murtaugh could have grown suspicious of the whole scene in China and thrown up his arms in surrender. Chery was first to market with his product and was undercutting him on price. In the first full year of sales, the QQ outsold the Spark by a ratio of five to one.

Chinese courts were ruling one way (in favor of Chery) when the facts pointed in the opposite direction. His own partner SAIC was a Chery shareholder, albeit reluctantly. The game appeared to be rigged against GM. But Murtaugh took stock of the situation and determined that the best thing to do was to forge ahead. In any enterprise, there are going to be reversals and upsets along the way. Sometimes the setbacks come as shocks. The test of one's mettle is in one's response to the adversity. There was another new car coming to Shanghai GM from Korea, the Excelle. Murtaugh was convinced that this product alone would soon alleviate some of the pain of the Chery QQ affair.

As for Yin, he remained quiet and congenial throughout the tense months following GM's discovery of the QQ. Chery promised not to do such a thing again, and it agreed not to export the car to any markets where the Spark was already on sale. Chery has since kept its word.

The self-effacing leader of Chery likes the role of the underdog. By 2010, his company would be producing more than six hundred thousand cars a year. Yet when asked by a reporter from the *Financial Times* in the autumn of that year when Chinese firms like Chery would be ready to compete with the global brands like Toyota, Honda, Buick, and Volkswagen, Yin replied in English: "Dozens of years."

The *Financial Times* reporter paused and then offered a polite correction: "You mean a dozen years, right?"

"No," Yin said with a straight face, "I mean dozens of years."

In 2003, the guys in charge at Shanghai GM worked with a much shorter time horizon—one that dealt not in dozens of years but in dozens of days.

15

PORSCHES AND SWEET POTATOES

Joseph Liu and his sales and marketing team at Shanghai General Motors had probably never met Linda Wang. But as Shanghai GM found itself reeling from Chery's blindside in early 2003, they would be forever grateful for Linda and other Chinese car buyers of her ilk. As they were to reveal, China's emerging wave of private car buyers were interested in much more than simply a small car at a cheap price.

Linda is a stylish, eccentric thirty-something Shanghai native who has been in the apparel business since finishing college. Her first job was with a multinational company sourcing products from China. Once she had mastered the essence of style, manufacturing, and pricing, Linda formed her own company and began designing, producing, and exporting clothes to the United States and Europe.

She poured her profits into the purchase of apartments in Shanghai. First, she bought a small two-bedroom place in the old French Quarter, down the street from where the city's party leaders lived. Then, she invested in a larger place in the Jing'An district. Next, she bought another apartment with more bedrooms and more bathrooms. Before long, Linda had collected half a dozen properties. She rented them—mostly to foreigners—for $1,500 to $5,000 per month. Her rental income alone soon climbed to $30,000 per month.

At the same time, the values of her Shanghai properties rose at head-turning speed. A unit acquired for $100,000 in 2000 was worth $220,000 by 2005. A larger place bought for $250,000 was now worth more than $500,000.

This attractive, hard-working, clever, tough young woman from Shanghai had leveraged her education and her street smarts to become independently wealthy by her mid-thirties.

"But what kind of car do you drive?" she was asked one day.

"No car. I don't want a car right now. There is no place to park, the traffic is terrible, and the taxi drivers are the worst. They would just dent my new car on the first day."

"Okay, but you are thinking about a car, right—maybe even an Audi or a BMW?"

"Audi or BMW?" she repeated dismissively. "No, when I get a car, it will be a Porsche."

"A Porsche. But, you know, a Porsche can run you more than $200,000 after import taxes."

Linda responded to the remark with a long silence. Then, perhaps because she was dealing with a foreigner, she felt compelled to explain. "Money," she said, "money is not a problem." *Qian bu shi wenti.*

Just a week after that conversation, Linda was walking down Huai Hai Road, one of Shanghai's most exclusive streets, with her mother and a friend. It was a cold, damp, winter afternoon, the kind with a chill that seeps into your bones and stays there.

Linda saw an older man stooping over a giant oil drum—his makeshift oven—baking sweet potatoes over hot coals. She turned to her companions and asked if they would like one. Then she approached the street vendor, ordered three potatoes and waited while he gave his wares one last turn over the coals. Then he wrapped them in paper, handed them over, and asked for payment.

Upon hearing the amount, the petite and charming Linda Wang lost her composure and began to shout: "How dare you try to charge me so much money! What, you think I just arrived from the countryside and know nothing? No, no, no. There's no way I'm paying that much for some stupid poor-quality potatoes!"

From a distance, Linda's companions saw that she was upset but could not hear above the din of traffic. But what could possibly be wrong, they asked?

"He's just a thief. Let's go away from here. Quickly. He wants to charge me 30 cents a potato when everyone in Shanghai who has a brain knows the price is only 25 cents. I have never in my life paid more than 25 cents for a potato, and I won't start now!"

The very same person who would not think twice about laying out $200,000 for a new Porsche felt strongly compelled to step on the neck of a poor sweet potato vendor, as if it were her civic duty! He would not get away with overcharging her. No way. Compassion is not a word found in the Chinese consumers' dictionary.

Not every prospective Chinese car buyer is independently wealthy, of course. And many Chinese, if told this story, would say: "Oh, but that is just how the small-minded Shanghai people act when money's involved." Still, the importance of branding to the Chinese consumer cannot be underestimated. When it comes to brand names, there is a spectrum from strength to weakness, and each point along the spectrum triggers a specific reaction. Brands with power can command a premium price that few Chinese will be inclined to haggle about. But woe unto those products without any brand strength, for they are at the mercy of a tough and unyielding consumer. The sweet-potato vendor, selling a basic commodity with no brand name, is destined to eke out a very meek existence.

Shanghai consumers may be tougher than their fellow countrymen, but they are not the exception when it comes to attitudes toward brands and the perceived value of products. This particular characteristic of Chinese consumers was not entirely apparent to Shanghai GM in 2003 as it prepared to launch the Excelle and the Spark. The thinking at the time was that China, like other developing markets, would demand small cars at low prices.

The common denominator for most emerging markets was *small and cheap*. From India to Brazil, from Thailand to Chile, the majority of consumers bought small, affordable cars. In India, for example, the best-selling car was a Suzuki Maruti, which started at just $5,500. In Brazil, most cars featured tiny engines that ran on ethanol.

Certainly, Chinese government officials would be able to tap into state budgets to buy larger cars like the Regal, Passat, or

Accord, cars that cost $40,000 or more. But private buyers would be a different story. Individual car buyers would be more likely to resemble the anxious administrator of Chapter Thirteen, desperately concerned about three dollars to cover the invoice for the paper cups.

This is why Chery's sleight of hand was such a blow to Shanghai GM. If the under-$10,000 segment were to become the fount of future growth, then what was Shanghai GM to do when a local competitor could bring a copycat product to market and undercut the Chevrolet Spark by 20 percent? Having lost one of their promising horses before the starting gates opened, the outlook for Shanghai GM was a little grim.

There were real concerns about the branding of the Excelle, too. Here was a Korean Daewoo product being rebadged as an American Buick sedan. At the time, Korean car quality was still considered a full notch below that of Japanese cars. Many of the essential parts were engineered and manufactured in Korea, too. Now the strategy was to ship those Korean parts to Shanghai, marry them with some other Chinese-made car parts, and call the end product a bright and shiny Buick. Would that approach really work?

Because consumers had come to equate Buick with its American heritage, the implicit message was that people who bought an Excelle were buying an "American" car. This was a gamble. If Chinese consumers learned that the Buick was essentially an American skin over a Daewoo from Korea, they might just stomp on the product with the same gusto that Linda Wang had stomped the sweet potato vendor.

David Chen had risen through the ranks to become GM's executive in charge of the Excelle launch in China. He felt that Shanghai GM could make the Korean-sourced Excelle a winner. To make the Daewoo more like a Buick, said Chen, they did major interior and exterior upgrades. Many people thought the experiment of putting a Buick brand name on a Korean car just would not work. But the cost of the alternative—a German-engineered Opel Astra rebadged as a Buick Excelle—was prohibitive. Murtaugh and Chen Hong backed the strategy to go with the Korean product.

There was a very real chance the whole strategy could backfire. But what choice did Shanghai GM have? They needed a low-cost car development base in Korea in order to stay price competitive. And they needed the Buick branding to preserve some pricing power. Once the decision was made, Shanghai GM president Chen Hong strongly advised his people to "stop arguing about the risks and get on with the job" of making the Excelle a success, according to people involved with the Excelle launch.

Soon after his arrival in 2001, Joseph Liu had identified three areas where Shanghai GM could improve its chances with the Chinese customer. First, and most important, was the engine size. The Buick engines were still too large for the Chinese. To get more customers into the showroom, the Buick Century (renamed the Regal when it was freshened at the end of 2002) would need to go from 6-cylinder engines to 4-cylinder engines and from 3 liters to less than 2.5 liters. Four-cylinder engines were enough to power the Passat, the Accord and even the big Audi A6.

It was a huge effort to repackage the Regal with a 4-cylinder engine because of continued resistance from skeptical Buick engineers in America who cringed at the thought of a 4-cylinder in a Buick. The Buick Excelle would also get a small engine—small, at least, by American standards. The compact car came with 1.6-liter and 1.8-liter engines as standard.

Beyond saving on fuel costs, Liu understood from his experience at GM in Taiwan that Chinese people cared a lot about the look and feel of the interior. The original Buick for China was handsome on the outside, but the dashboard, seats, and trim were utilitarian, almost devoid of a human touch. In focus group studies, some even referred to the Buick's instrument panel as "a carcass." To improve, the interior had to be warmer and friendlier, with more attention to detail. Here is where the Germans, and the Japanese especially, enjoyed a big edge—they paid very close attention to the interior.

Third, Liu knew that he had to get dealers on his side, which meant he and has staff would begin treating them as equals. His first step as the new head of marketing and sales at Shanghai GM was to invite all Buick dealers to a sales planning conference where Shanghai GM would share new product plans and market forecasts for the coming year. He told his people to line up and greet each dealer as they entered the large auditorium.

His staff recoiled. "What? Why would we want to stand in line and welcome them? They're just suppliers!" Liu staffers had previously lumped parts suppliers and dealers into a single category: lowly service providers, subservient to the mighty Shanghai GM.

Liu told the dealers: "Look, you're my partners; I am here to work with you to make money." That show of respect got the dealers' attention.

Not long after the Excelle launch in August 2003, a strange and wonderful thing happened. Buick dealers began reporting strong demand not only for the low-end version of the Excelle but also for the fully loaded, most expensive version. Chinese buyers were embracing the Buick brand, overlooking the car's Korean origins, and spending money on the top-of-the-line Excelle. The most popular Excelle was a version that cost more than $20,000.

What made this demand so striking was that among the Buick buyers were not only government officials but also private businesses, joint-venture companies, and individuals. This new wave of car buyers wanted large cars with smaller engines. There were, clearly, many more Linda Wangs out there than anyone had ever expected.

Then the leaders at Shanghai GM noticed another development; an unexpected gift: Chinese buyers were lining up to buy the new Buick Regal, which had undergone vast improvements to both the interior and exterior at the end of 2002. It also featured a 2.5-liter engine, which was key to capturing more government purchases. The smaller the engine size, the more city and provincial officials would qualify to buy a Buick, according to rules set down by the central government.

Even global automotive industry leaders like Toyota got caught flat-footed. When the Japanese colossus entered the market in 2003, it first introduced the Vios, a subcompact. Chinese buyers yawned at the offering, wondered why one of the world's best car companies had shipped such a bland little car to the market, and gave it a pass. Ford, too, misread the market. It led with the Fiesta, a tiny subcompact from Europe with a basic interior and, what Ford thought most important, a low price. Again, Chinese consumers puzzled over the choice of offerings from Ford and largely ignored the car.

The Chinese propensity to spend so lavishly on cars did not make any sense to Toyota, Ford, or many expert economists or forecasters. China's per-capita gross domestic product had galloped upward since the 1980s, but the average annual income was still only $1,000. That categorized China as of one of the poorest countries on earth. Never in the history of the automobile had a country with such low average income exhibited such emphatic demand for bigger, relatively expensive cars.

Market analysts searched vigorously for evidence of financial tricks or bubbles or corruption to explain the strange phenomenon. But none could be found. Somehow, Chinese private buyers were coming up with cash to make full payments for cars priced twenty, thirty, even forty times the nation's average yearly incomes.

In 2003, the average price of a new car in India was $6,000. In China, the figure was $23,000, even though the two countries had roughly the same GDP per capita, around $1,000. It was an early indication of the accelerating concentration of wealth in one sector of Chinese society. Owners of private businesses like Ms. Wang's were amassing small fortunes. If marketers had looked hard enough, they might have picked up some clues from China's luxury-car segment. Demand for luxury cars in China was upside-down, or the inverse of what one found in other markets, even developed markets like the United States.

In America and in Germany, sales volumes are correlated to price points, as one might expect. The C-Class, the most affordable Mercedes sedan, sells best. The E-Class, a larger and more expensive car, is the second-strongest seller in the lineup. And the flagship S-Class, a large and very exclusive car, contributes the smallest number of Mercedes sales each year. But in China, the order was reversed. The S-Class, which started at more than $140,000, was the best seller, followed by the E-Class, then the C-Class.

Buying a luxury car was all about making a statement. Showing up at the Sheshan Country Club in an E-Class told your friends that business was just so-so. Driving up in a diminutive C-Class indicated that you might be in real financial trouble. If you were any sort of self-respecting businessman, you just had to be in the S-Class.

But that was the luxury segment, where total sales were in the range of only a few thousand cars per year. It was much more difficult to understand how so many other customers could afford cars like the Accord or the Passat or the Regal, priced at $30,000 and more. Were private buyers getting easy loans from banks for their businesses and then spending the money on cars instead?

Or could it be that car dealers were secretly financing the purchases in order to reach sales targets that would trigger bonuses? And if so, would the whole thing collapse like a house of cards?

Was it possible that private buyers could get money from government officials to purchase the expensive cars in their own names and then give the cars to the officials for their private use?

This was China: a place and time where everything is possible but nothing is obvious or easy. Even so, sometimes it's necessary to resign yourself to developments beyond comprehension and just go with it, whatever "it" may be.

That's basically what the leaders at Shanghai GM were doing in 2003. "Never mind the 'why.' Let's just concentrate on meeting this outrageously strong demand for cars we can make profits on." And the profits were huge. "We are making more money than God," a senior executive at General Motors China said in private at the time.

The sales results in 2003 were nothing short of spectacular. Shanghai GM sold an astonishing 89,900 Regals, up from 37,000 the year before. The Buick Excelle had a strong first year, achieving sales of 36,000 cars since its launch in August. Sales of the GL8 minivan, the Buick Sail and the Chevy Spark had all kicked up a notch, too.

In the short time span between 2000 and 2003, Shanghai GM's sales had rocketed from just 30,000 to 200,000 cars and minivans. To make full use of the factory, Jack Smith had asked for 100,000 units in 2002. But Shanghai GM delivered 200,000 the very next year! Now the company found itself needing to add production capacity in order to handle the surging demand.

Finally, after years of wrenching internal battles and external shocks, Shanghai GM was hitting its stride. The dealers were happily making nice money. Chinese customers—both individuals and government—were growing more and more enchanted by the Buick brand.

Just about the only worry was how to increase production capacity to meet the stunning spurt in demand for new Buicks. That was a good problem to have, given that exclusivity and waiting times tended to fuel Chinese auto buyers' desire.

As the Chinese like to say: amid such rosy conditions, the future is very bright.

16

GETTING THEIR ARMS
AROUND CHINA

As 2004 got under way, Phil Murtaugh remained humble about the breakthrough growth and profits of Shanghai GM the previous year. There was still much work to be done, he knew. China had opened the car market to full competition only a year earlier. Now all of the world's best carmakers were pouring in to form new joint ventures. Shanghai GM would need to move very quickly and very smartly to hold off the avalanche of new challengers.

What he may or may not have anticipated was that the greatest challenges would come from within his own company. The China business had become too large for Detroit's hands-off approach to continue.

Chairman and CEO Rick Wagoner decided it was time to get the company's arms around China, that vast and inscrutable market so far from headquarters.

Murtaugh was still focused on making Shanghai GM a winner. He had worked hard to build a spirit of cooperation with his partner SAIC. There had been no shortage of trials and tribulations. There was the red-faced moment during the launch of the Century when Jack Smith could not find the brake release. The unwelcome news that cross-town rival Shanghai VW would build the Passat, a direct competitor to the Century. The difficult, drawn-out arguments with German engineers over coatings for body panels and engine types. The messy jousting within the GM family for the car that eventually became the Buick Sail. The startling move by

Chery to bring the QQ to market before the Chevrolet Spark was even launched.

Despite these hardships, Murtaugh continued to believe in the strength that came from a solid team. When asked later how GM and SAIC tended to divide responsibilities within the joint venture, Murtaugh was quick to reply: "No, no. We did not divide things up like that. It was a team."

To sustain momentum and build comradeship among his closest lieutenants, Murtaugh would host the occasional game of pool at his home in Pudong. There would be no shortage of cigars and beers and even some American music on the portable stereo system. The games—played on a small, slightly worn table and with cues that showed some mileage—were never very serious either. The gathering was just an opportunity to relax, enjoy some laughs, and strengthen the bonds between people, most of whom were thousands of miles from home.

If someone was invited but did not show up, though, they could expect a call: "Hey, where are you? We are all here waiting and you have not shown up yet. Don't give me any bull about being busy with work. Get over here!" Murtaugh was not one to take no for an answer.

American employees assigned to Shanghai GM found the GM culture in China very different from the one back in the States. "I worked hard, very hard. But I enjoyed it," is how a young engineer named Mark Miller put it. Miller, on a three-year assignment from the United States, did not mind the ten-hour days at the office and the after-dinner conference calls with Germany and Detroit. He explained, "Phil was the kind of leader who did not demand respect. He earned it. He led by example. He did not care about titles or how you dressed, as long as you did your job well. Our motto was work hard, play hard."

For Miller and many at Shanghai GM, the number one outlet for "playing hard" was the golf course. China had witnessed an explosion in golf since 2000, and there were more than a dozen high-quality country clubs to choose from in the Shanghai area, where green fees routinely topped $100.

When not on the course, American executives at Shanghai GM often bonded at one of their favorite watering holes—places like the Big Bamboo, the Blue Frog, or O'Malley's—or gathered at a friend's home for a theme party.

The Chinese people liked Murtaugh, too. He did not speak many words of Chinese. But he connected with Chinese executives and government officials on a personal level. They admired and even enjoyed his bluntness. When things got hot and he flew into a brief rage, they still sensed that he had everyone's best interest at heart.

Even the most hardened financial types at GM headquarters back in Detroit had to acknowledge Murtaugh's head-turning results. Near the back of GM's annual report for 2003, one could find the profits made by its subsidiary in China: $435 million! At a time when GM in North America was offering $5,000 rebates to people who would buy their cars, Shanghai GM was turning a tidy profit of $4,000 per car.

When the earnings number appeared in the media, Murtaugh received a note of congratulations from a friend in the business. Murtaugh replied with some self-deprecating humor: "Even a blind squirrel eventually finds a nut."

Back at Detroit headquarters, executives were genuinely hoping to stumble upon a domestic nut somewhere, somehow. At the start of 2004, their outlook was increasingly bleak. General Motors was fighting a losing battle with the unions—line workers were still earning $70 an hour in wages and benefits. And GM was coming up short in the contest for buyers, too. Despite record discounts and rebates, GM was still losing market share to the Japanese.

As things turned out, 2004 was the last year in which GM would make a profit. And 70 percent of that profit came from GMAC, its financial arm, which had aggressively pursued the residential mortgage business. GM was in deep trouble. It was time to do something—anything—to change the company's direction.

Decades earlier and on a different continent, Bertolt Brecht had written *The Threepenny Opera,* a satire about power and society. "The people no longer approve of the government," went one of the lines. "It is time to find a new people."

Now, it was clear that the North American customer no longer approved of GM. In such a situation, what was management to do?

What GM needed, declared chairman and CEO Rick Wagoner in 2004, was a worldwide reporting matrix. As he surveyed GM's global empire, he saw far too much redundancy. Some markets were off doing their own thing—too independent. It was necessary to bring everyone into the same global system. And the person to do that at GM was one Troy Clarke.

Clarke had what the business world calls a "strong executive presence." He was tall, spoke with confidence, and was articulate with the facts of his company. But he also exhibited a hint of the "friendly arrogance" that Steven Rattner had called endemic in the ranks of GM executives.

Clarke had developed a reputation within GM for going into awkward situations and making things right. First, as president of GM do Mexico in the late 1990s, he was able to erase years of ill will between the Mexican unions and GM management by respectfully listening to the workers and making adjustments. Based on that success, Wagoner asked him to take the lead for GM through difficult negotiations with the United Auto Workers in 2003.

In 2004, Clarke was appointed to lead GM Asia-Pacific operations. In June, Rick Wagoner announced that GM's Asia-Pacific headquarters would move from Singapore to China. "Establishing our regional headquarters in Shanghai recognizes how important China has become to our plans to expand our global industry leadership," Wagoner said. "Having a strong presence in this dynamic and growing market is not an option anymore. It's a necessity."

GM China's growth under Murtaugh had made the move a necessity. By 2004, China accounted for 85 percent of GM sales in Asia. Murtaugh would become a victim of his own success.

Singapore was a six-hour flight south of Shanghai. It had been the base for GM Asia-Pacific headquarters since the early 1990s. Compared to China, Singapore might as well have been on a different planet. Average incomes in Singapore were already higher than those in the United Kingdom, and the airport and mass transit systems were among the most advanced in the world. People there spoke fluent English; the streets were spotless, the shopping malls elegant.

It was a beautiful place for senior executives to live and work. However, situating GM Asia-Pacific headquarters in Singapore was like presiding over African markets from Geneva. It was not even remotely connected to the action. What would the shareholders say?

So it was decided that Clarke and all of his Singapore staff would be moved to Shanghai by the end of 2004. The GM Asia-Pacific operations would set up less than a mile from the GM China and Shanghai GM offices, in the heart of the exclusive Lu Jia Zui district, along the Pudong River on the east side of Shanghai.

For the eight years since his start in China, Phil Murtaugh had always reported to bosses in Singapore, that faraway island. And he had always been given a lot of leeway to run things as he saw fit. But from this point on, GM China would be absorbed by—and take directions from—the GM Asia-Pacific organization just down the street. When Murtaugh's boss, GM Asia-Pacific president Fritz Henderson, left Asia in 2004 to take charge of GM Europe, Murtaugh somewhat wistfully recalled the respect and autonomy he had enjoyed under Henderson: "Fritz used to ask what the situation was, and then how I recommended to take care of it." It was an autonomy he would no longer enjoy under the new regime.

When a China business unit of an American company performs exceptionally well, the top management at headquarters sometimes salutes the efforts with recognition and redoubles support of the team on the front lines. New investment, a larger head count, and more authority. Sometimes, but not always. More often, headquarters pursues a different avenue of thinking, one that goes like this: *Geez, that China market is really taking off—it's much more than we ever expected. Now, wait, who do we have over there, again? Oh, yeah, that's right. Well, the footprint over there is getting pretty big now. We really need to get our arms around that.*

Get our arms around that. Translation: *Take control.*

The auto industry has no monopoly on this sudden urge for headquarters to get its arms around things in China. From white goods to electronics to apparel to sports equipment, from accounting to investment banking, the story is the same. Send someone into the new market until that market becomes large enough and palatable enough for the "right caliber" of people to enter and take charge. That's the time to send in the A Team.

Imagine the scene: A senior executive is put in charge of GM's Asia-Pacific markets. China accounts for 80 to 85 percent of the business. There is already a guy in charge of the China business, and he's been there for eight years, doing a superb job. He works in an office just a couple of blocks away.

What will that leave the big boss to do—focus on the remaining small markets, the crumbs? That just won't do. What would GM leadership back in Detroit say?

Of course, a newly arrived executive (like Clarke) will not just charge in and start making changes. Before taking action, it will be important to first conduct some due diligence. There are probably lots of questions. In this case, that meant second-guessing Murtaugh's approach to advancing GM's interests in China.

A former colleague recalled, "Phil had a way of dealing with the Chinese. They liked him. Then [Clarke] came in and started saying to Phil: 'You need to tell the Chinese to do more of this and less of that.' Well, you just don't 'tell the Chinese'—that doesn't work." The Chinese, let it not be forgotten, control the licenses.

It was the fall of 2004 when Clarke had lunch with suppliers at the Grand Hyatt Hotel in downtown Shanghai. "Phil keeps telling us that Shanghai GM is the poster child of U.S.–China business relations," Clarke said. He let the statement hang in the air, like a question that needed an answer, and then changed the subject. Murtaugh appeared to be too close to GM's Chinese partners for the corporation's liking. Now there was a new sheriff in town, and he was going to do things differently.

With the new global matrix reporting, GM's operations in China would be moved to the same (sinking) boat as the rest of the company. Recommendations about how to run China would come down through the ranks—recommendations that "had zero relevance in China," said a GM employee who was posted in Shanghai at the time.

Phil Murtaugh was never long on patience. He had a business to take care of. In May 2004, demand for cars in China slowed abruptly. The government had given directives to banks to curtail lending in order to avoid runaway economic growth. GM was not alone in being affected by this. For the first time since the height of the Asian financial crisis in 1998, demand for cars of all makes and models in China had gone soft.

When a supplier dropped by to tell Murtaugh that his company had just bought a new Regal in June, Murtaugh said: "That's the best news I've had all month." There was no telling when the red-hot demand of 2003 and early 2004 might resume.

Putting the brakes on lending should not have had such a quick and dramatic impact on the car market. After all, car loans still figured in less than 10 percent of total sales in China. Customers preferred to pay in cash. But restricted lending did hit businesses, state enterprises, and private companies alike. The flow of cheap working capital loans that many companies had been redirecting into car purchases had been shut off.

As sales momentum slowed to a crawl, some car companies cut prices or offered discounts. But this action seemed to backfire. The Chinese consumer concluded that price cuts meant that the carmakers were in trouble. If they waited long enough, the con-sumer's thinking went, the carmakers would be forced into making additional price cuts.

Even through the uncertain summer market of 2004, Shanghai GM did not slow the pace of its expansion into new areas of business. The Cadillac brand was formally launched in June at an epic event inside the Forbidden City in Beijing. And in August, GM and SAIC finalized a new joint venture, GMAC-SAIC Automotive Finance Co., Ltd., to provide loans to future Shanghai GM car buyers. The financing company was a crucial addition, as it was still unclear how much longer the market could grow at such a blazing clip without car loans.

By autumn 2004, the government seemed satisfied that the economy was back under control, so it allowed banks to resume lending. The market came back strongly, and by year's end, Shanghai GM sales had grown nearly 33 percent, from 204,000 to 267,000 units. SGM had almost tripled its sales from the 2002 level of 112,000 cars. Excelle sales leapt to 92,000, up from 37,000 the year before.

In spite of the slowdown that started in May and lasted through Shanghai's sticky humid summer, 2004 ended up as another incred-ibly good year for Shanghai GM. The outlook for 2005 was even brighter. Shanghai GM was planning for another year of torrid growth with sales expected to climb again by 30 percent.

These were high times for Shanghai GM.

Yet Murtaugh was chafing under the constant questioning from the higher-ups. He had to battle with people in the matrix over crucial things like which product was right for China. These were people who barely knew where to find China on a map. Murtaugh was second-guessed time and again, despite his strong track record building the GM business in China.

So, just ninety days into 2005, with Shanghai GM once again enjoying explosive growth, Murtaugh decided to stop working for General Motors. He was done as chairman and CEO of General Motors China. He was done with GM, after thirty years. He was leaving Shanghai GM—a company that, since his arrival eight years earlier, had developed into a $6 billion enterprise.

Once word leaked out that Murtaugh had resigned, there was a media frenzy. The Chinese could hardly believe their eyes when they read the news of his departure. "I heard some talk that they were going to bring him back to Detroit," said a former colleague.

Clarke quickly named Kevin Wale, an Australian, to succeed Murtaugh. Wale had been the chairman of Vauxhall Motors, the GM subsidiary in the United Kingdom. Everyone at Shanghai GM was wondering the same thing: *How will Wale handle the transition, especially the delicate relations with the Chinese partners at SAIC? And what will become of Shanghai GM after Murtaugh?*

PART FOUR

QUICK ACCELERATION, THEN A TIGHT CORNER

17

THE BEST AND WORST
OF TIMES

In the chaotic weeks following the news of his resignation as chairman of General Motors China in March 2005, everyone wanted to talk to Phil Murtaugh. Competing car companies wanted him. Blue-chip parts suppliers wanted him. Private equity guys, with their deep pockets, joined the pursuit too.

Murtaugh was so highly regarded in China that Starbucks reportedly made him an offer to become chairman of the company's thriving business there. But the forty-nine-year-old Murtaugh was, for the time being, content to spend time at his home in Shanghai, reflect on his thirty years at GM, and think about what should come next.

An excerpt from an interview that summer with Keith Bradsher, Hong Kong bureau chief of the *New York Times*, captured Murtaugh's sentiment and his sense of humor:

> Mr. Murtaugh said that he was playing a little golf now, but found himself with many idle hours. "I'm looking for work," he said, and then joked, "do you have a deck that needs painting?"

One day he was contacted by a group of investors from New York with an intriguing proposition: How would Phil Murtaugh like to run the show at Geely Motors?

Geely was a young and fast-growing Chinese car company based in Hangzhou, about eighty miles from Shanghai. Already listed on the Hong Kong stock exchange, the company was working to raise more capital from private equity investors in the United States. The American investors would feel much more comfortable funding Geely with a Westerner in charge.

Murtaugh agreed to meet with Li Shufu, Geely's billionaire founder, who, as a teenager, had dropped out of school and started building companies. He had made his way up the value chain from home appliances to motorcycle parts to complete motorcycles and eventually, in 1997, to cars. His company's vision was declared on large red banners in the rafters of the final assembly plant: "Build affordable cars for the masses!"

Li was a native of a farming village near Taizhou, in central Zhejiang province, far away from the big cities and the sophisticated city slickers in Shanghai and Beijing. But Zhejiang entrepreneurs like Li are considered the most fearless and cunning business people in China. Businessmen from Shanghai tremble at the mention of Zhejiang people, especially those from Wenzhou and Taizhou.

So their initial meeting was set up. Murtaugh clearly understood the nuances of personal rapport in China. He listened carefully to the advice about Li from the money guys:

- Feel free to talk about anything with Li.
- He's a smart guy and will be quick to get your message.
- He prefers to speak Chinese but understands English very well.
- It's not easy for him, as founder, to give up some control. But he knows that's the price of getting more funding.
- Just one thing: Please do not mention anything about his background—you know, as coming from the countryside. You know, *nongmin* (farmer) does not have a good meaning in China.

There was nervous tension as Murtaugh, escorted by the private equity champions, strode in to find Li inside the teahouse in Shanghai. Murtaugh spoke first. "Hello, Mr. Li," he said with a firm handshake. "I understand that you're a farmer."

The private equity guys felt their knees buckle. They were stunned. Did Murtaugh just say what they thought they heard him say? What in the world was he thinking? This surely would kill the deal immediately!

Everyone, including Li, was silent in the seconds that followed. Then, with a glint in his eye, Murtaugh completed his opening salvo: "Me too. I grew up on a farm in Ohio."

With that, everyone broke into relieved laughter. With a modicum of words, Murtaugh had set the tone and the no-nonsense terms of engagement. Li may or may not have liked what he heard. But it was hard not to respect Phil Murtaugh.

When Murtaugh departed from GM China, many expected a rupture in the company's operations. But there was no immediate cataclysmic implosion at Shanghai General Motors. The aftershocks from this abrupt shifting of GM's tectonic plates would not be felt until four years later—in the spring and summer of 2009.

In the mid-1990s, ten years earlier, Murtaugh and his team had been given a lot of leeway to build a joint venture in a far-away place called China. Aside from Chairman Jack Smith, Rick Swando, David Chen, and a few others in the company, most people at GM either had no interest in China or were simply flat out against going there at all. Then, much to the surprise of many, the China experiment started to work. The joint venture was profit-able on an operating basis in its first year, and it even started paying dividends back to America in 2002, just four years into operation.

Then in 2004, with China making record sales and profits, came the decision to move GM's Asia-Pacific operations center from Singapore to Shanghai. At the same time, folks working for GM in China must have been aware of the dismal direction of the company as it was being run from Detroit. Market share in North America, the company's most important market, was down. Losses were in the billions of dollars every quarter.

There was bound to be a collision when the parent, GM, came to "get its arms around" the overly independent child, Shanghai GM. But the child had already grown up into a young adult, proud of its accomplishments.

Said one GM executive, "The official line was that we were moving the office from Singapore to Shanghai to get closer to the market. But I have my own theories about what was behind the move." The operation in China had grown too large, too profitable, and too independent. It needed to be brought back into the GM corporate fold.

When Murtaugh tendered his resignation, perhaps he was simply throwing his hands up in the air. If he expressed what he was thinking— "I thought our orders were to make the joint venture a success"—no one could claim to misunderstand.

Few people, if any, saw it coming. "I know there must have been some disputes between Phil and Troy [Clarke]," recalls one supplier. "But no one ever thought Murtaugh would leave. Everyone knew he built the company."

In the back of everyone's mind was what impact the change at the top would have on the relationship with the Chinese leaders from SAIC. Chairman Hu Maoyuan and SGM president Chen Hong had worked shoulder to shoulder with Murtaugh and his team from the very start, including the negotiations to form the joint venture. How would they react to Murtaugh's replacement, Kevin Wale? There were some rocky moments at the beginning. "I'm not sure when Kevin came in he was aware of what he was getting into," said one executive who worked under both Murtaugh and Wale.

There was speculation that Murtaugh might even be hired to lead SAIC's quest for its own sedan, under the Roewe brand name. The Chinese, though, are seldom inclined to show their hand right away in awkward situations. They are even less likely to take some overt action. Their preferred course of action is to wait and watch patiently to see what will come next from the other party—and then respond accordingly.

In cases where the Chinese get genuinely angry about something, a favored approach is to "go dark" or become inaccessible. They are no longer available for meetings, no matter what time of day or night. They don't decline requests for a meeting directly; they are more likely to use a go-between: a secretary. Kerry Ivan had experienced a mild form of this behavior at Beijing Jeep back in the 1980s. But the avoidance strategy is still common today. When you can't find your Chinese partner for a talk, well, you can be sure there is a problem.

But SAIC did not shut the door. They kept the channels open, offered the standard platitudes about preserving a good relationship, watched, and waited.

A Chinese executive from a rival company offered this assessment of SAIC's stance: "They will look for the new guy from GM to do one of two things. If he comes in as a hard-charger and tries to impose his will, he will break the bonds. Things will deteriorate rapidly. Or if, on the other hand, he is too soft, too careful to be respectful of the relationship, then the Chinese will surely interpret it as a sign of some weakness. Then Chinese will occupy more ground in the joint venture."

Occupying more ground in a 50–50 joint venture means taking effective control. With Murtaugh no longer present to look after GM's interest in the tough daily give-and-take negotiations with the partner, the power in an equal joint venture could begin to shift to one side.

"Phil was like a battlefield commander, very hands on," said a GM employee who worked closely with Murtaugh. His were tough shoes to fill. There was bound to be some awkward moments as Wale took over as president of GM China in May 2005. Both men maintained memberships at the Tianma Country Club golf course, about an hour west of downtown Shanghai. A few dozen ranking executives from GM China and Shanghai GM played there regularly, too. One month they were saluting Murtaugh as their leader; the next month they were greeting their new boss, arriving from Australia via England. Who do you go out for a round with—your old boss or your new boss?

Wale had been involved in Asia-Pacific business planning for China in the late 1990s when he worked from Singapore. He knew the basics of China business activities, but he still would need to ease into things as smoothly as possible. And he would need some luck on his side, too. Anyone in his position would.

A once-in-a-lifetime stroke of luck arrived just when GM needed it most. Starting in 2005, China was on its way to the most spectacular car market boom the world has ever seen. In hindsight, 2005 marked a year in which GM's universe of business resembled two freight trains gaining speed in opposite directions. There was the "southbound" freight train in the United States, destined to end up in a spectacular crash four years later. And there was the "northbound" freight train, China, rolling at ever-higher speeds towards car market nirvana.

The market numbers illustrate how quickly and dramatically the freight trains rolled in opposite directions. The U.S. car and truck market dropped like a stone, from 17 million units in 2005 to just 10 million in 2009. In China, the market roared from 3.6 million in 2005 to 10.5 million cars in 2009. By the end of 2009, China had become the number one car market in the world. In the space of less than sixty months, the world's two largest car markets experienced a sales volume swing of 14 million cars and trucks!

China's towering market was no car loan bubble. Incredibly, 90 percent of car sales in China in 2009 were still settled in cash. The growth in 2009 was so spectacular that some analysts speculated that the government must have been buying cars (as a kind of stimulus program) and storing them away in warehouses. But dealers on the ground knew the demand was real.

While GM in Detroit was rattling down the tracks toward insolvency, in China the automakers, suppliers, and dealers were raking in record profits. Shanghai GM more than doubled sales, from 356,000 in 2005 to 787,000 units in 2009.

While GM in Detroit would soon be on its way to closing factories and dealerships across America, Shanghai GM was working overtime to find and appoint new dealers and build more factories.

But back in 2005, China's sustained, torrid growth to come was still unforeseen. Murtaugh's departure came at a very bad time. China was the only place in the GM world that did not look like a black hole. North America was losing money. Europe was losing money. Investments in other strategic markets—India and Thailand—were not delivering to the level expected.

In America, the problem was not one of a weak consumer appetite. The U.S. car market, as measured by sales of cars and trucks, was still running strong. Sales for the year would come to seventeen million cars and trucks, one of the highest in history. The real problem was paltry demand for *GM* cars and trucks. American consumers enjoyed the richest menu of car choices in the world—and the majority of buyers were crossing GM off their shopping list.

GM in 2005 was losing billions of dollars. GM's market share continued its decline. UAW wages and benefits, against all logic, stayed as lofty as ever.

GM was saddled with more than one million cars in inventory, mostly parked on dealer lots around the country. The attitude among GM leaders in Detroit—so vividly depicted in Paul Ingrassia's book *Crash Course: The American Automobile Industry's Road from Glory to Disaster*—was part embarrassment, part denial. One fact was undeniable: General Motors, the largest carmaker in the world, was making a record number of cars that people in North America did not want.

In shining contrast, GM's business in China was just about to take off. In fact, Shanghai GM was already soaring. In 2005, Chinese sales of Buicks, Chevrolets, and Cadillacs reached 356,000 cars, up 33 percent from the year before. GM had never before enjoyed such dramatic sales increases in any other overseas market.

The Buick Excelle was by far the most popular car, accounting for more than four out of ten GM sales in China. The 2002 acquisition of Daewoo—where the Excelle was designed and developed—was proving to be a mighty success. David Chen had been right to recommend the Korean source for the Excelle.

The Excelle was not a "looker"; it would not catch your eye as it passed on the street. But Chinese consumers did not find dramatic lines alluring. Instead, they got satisfaction from a basic four-door sedan with soft rounded corners and neutral colors like silver or gray or champagne or white. Buick Excelle buyers came mainly from the surging numbers of young urban professionals who wanted a reliable commuter car and an admired brand name, at a reasonable price. Interior space counted—they liked to have room for their whole family, including the grandparents. They cared a lot about gas mileage, too.

When rejecting a car model, Chinese like to say: "That car, I can buy it. But I just can't maintain it." Maintaining refers to any costs after purchase, including—and especially—the cost of filling the tank with gasoline. Linda Wang types might not hesitate to shell out $200,000 for a new Porsche. But they cannot stand spending a dime more than is necessary on gasoline.

Not every GM product was a success in China, however. Cadillac managed to find only 801 buyers for its CTS sedan in 2005. The CTS, Cadillac's smallest car, offered many features that

Chinese buyers did not want. For starters, the design of the CTS was inspired by the bold, sharp lines of the U.S. Air Force stealth fighter jet. Whereas Chinese like rounded corners, the new Cadillac design was all edges.

Second, the CTS came with a larger engine than the competition. Chinese buyers quickly relegated the CTS to the same category as their (dated) image of gas-guzzling Cadillacs. But the final nail in the coffin of the CTS was its cramped interior. The driver's seat was like a cockpit, and there was very little legroom in the back seat. Chinese luxury car buyers like space. Big is good. Giant is better.

A GM Cadillac executive working on the CTS launch was in a Shanghai Cadillac showroom one afternoon when a prospective buyer showed up. The customer walked back and forth across the floor a couple of times, allowing himself only small glances at the CTS.

Then a Cadillac sales consultant approached: "How can I help you, sir?"

"Well, I came to look at a Cadillac. Where are they?" the customer asked. The sales consultant extended her arm in the direction of the shiny new CTS in the middle of the showroom, just a few feet away.

"Oh, no," said the customer. "That's not a Cadillac. It's too small."

Weak interest in the CTS was a small blemish for GM China, like not getting the extra-credit answer right on an exam that you've already aced.

But Chevrolet's strong first year quickly made everyone forget about Cadillac's struggles. One of Murtaugh's final contributions before his departure was the formal launch of the Chevrolet brand in China. In January of 2005, Shanghai GM announced plans to appoint a hundred dealers nationwide and introduce several new Chevrolet products to the China market.

Chevrolet's first-year results were very encouraging. The original Buick Sail (now rebadged as a Chevrolet Sail), the subcompact Aveo, and the Epica (an intermediate-size sedan) totaled more than eighty thousand sales for the year.

The strong start was important because Chevrolet was positioned to appeal to China's emerging middle-class buyers. A popular

Chevrolet brand for the middle class would free up Buick to retain its premium positioning: a car for the affluent.

Chinese consumers hold the Buick brand, as an American icon, in high esteem. When asked why she chose a Buick Regal over the Honda Accord or Toyota Camry, one young Chinese professional in Shanghai was direct: "More respect when I pull up in front of a hotel."

GM in China had a lot going for it. Wale was stepping into a position that was both delicate and very promising. Although it would be tough for anyone to fill the shoes of the much-liked Murtaugh, the basic building blocks for Shanghai GM's future growth were all in place.

Buick, Cadillac, and Chevrolet brands had each been established. There was a new joint venture with SAIC to provide car loans to future buyers. Shanghai GM in 2005 also became the market share leader in China—surpassing Shanghai VW for the first time. Sales momentum was never better.

When he took over as president of GM China in May, Wale quickly sized up the situation: "We were doing okay. We just needed to work out how to grow as fast as China." One of the biggest challenges the company faced, he would later say, was "getting an exact forecast" of how big the China car market would get. Demand for new cars would get huge in a hurry, making even the most optimistic forecasts look ridiculously conservative.

For Wale, the hot market meant that there were many things to do:

- Nurture relations with the partner.
- Build a network of dealers for the newly launched Chevrolet.
- Strengthen the performance of SAIC-GM-Wuling, a joint venture in southern China making micro vans and micro trucks.
- Grow GMAC's financing business.
- Enhance Cadillac product offerings.
- Plan new products.
- Recruit and hire good people.

There was no end to the list.

As Wale said, the "challenge was to grow as fast" as demand. During his first sixty days, Wale got a sense of just how fast China could move. He presided over the opening of car and engine plants and the launch of the all-new Chevrolet Aveo. In May 2005, Shanghai GM began production at its second plant in Shanghai. In June, SAIC-GM-Wuling purchased a new plant in Qingdao to make Wuling-brand micro cars. Also that month, SAIC, GM, and Shanghai GM started engine production at a new plant in Shandong province. Then in early July, Shanghai GM launched the Chevrolet Aveo hatchback.

The Shanghai GM joint venture was strong and getting stronger, seemingly by the day. The company would need to build out the Chevrolet dealership network. The marketing and sales aces at Shanghai GM would take on the Chevrolet dealer network expansion. Joseph Liu, the gifted and knowledgeable executive recruited by Murtaugh from Taiwan, had built a very strong marketing team. Buick dealers had been making money, and this would make it easier to attract new dealers for Chevrolet.

Looking at Shanghai GM's seemingly endless to-do list, it was evident there was a lot of work to be done to keep pace with growing demand. However, because Murtaugh had left foundations in place to meet the many challenges of this exploding market, Wale was free to turn his main attention to a smaller, lesser-known Chinese joint venture. One in which GM owned a 34-percent share.

18

MINIATURE VEHICLES

"Lou told us to go take a look," recalled GM North America manufacturing manager Larry Zahner, referring to his former boss, Louis Hughes. The year was 1997, and Zahner and his colleague, Frank Chou, flew fifty-five minutes from Guangzhou to Liuzhou, a way off-the-beaten-track town in Guangxi province.

From Liuzhou, it was another two-hour ride in a van over bumpy roads to the Wuling plant. "It wasn't Mandarin, it wasn't Cantonese, it wasn't Shanghainese, not sure what it was they were speaking. So, even Frank, who's Chinese, had trouble when we stopped to ask for directions," said Zahner.

What Zahner and Chou found in Wuling that day was a rudimentary plant making miniature trucks and vans. The business had begun in 1985, with technical assistance from Mitsubishi. Its products ranged in price from $3,000 to $6,000. In 1998, the Liuzhou mini vehicle factory was renamed Liuzhou Wuling Motors.

Just as Korea had developed into a stable and reliable center for intermediate-priced cars, Wuling might be able to provide more small cars at even lower prices. Equally important, Wuling represented a channel to the huge number of Chinese consumers who lived and worked in the countryside. The factory was using manufacturing methods dating from long, long ago. "They were drilling blanks with hand tools," marveled Zahner. This technique had not been used in the United States for decades.

They also found that Wuling was making money. That made an impression, too. Here was this company in the middle of nowhere in China, landlocked inside one of China's poorest provinces, and the guys in charge had figured out ways to make a profit on small vehicles.

There was a lot going on for GM in China in 1997, with the launch of the Shanghai GM joint venture just around the corner, as well as efforts to make sense of the star-crossed Jinbei GM truck joint venture in Shenyang. So, making an investment in Wuling was not a top priority. But Zahner, who in 1998 would be named president of GM China, liked what he saw. "I felt that it [Wuling] was going to be something good for GM one day," he said later.

When it was time to leave after two days of visiting the plant and its management team, Zahner made a spontaneous gesture. He took one of his business cards from his pocket, tore it in two, put half of the card back in his pocket and gave the other half to Shen Yang, the general manager of Wuling Motors. Then he said: "I hope one day we find a way to get our companies together and then we can make my business card into a single piece again."

It was in China's backcountry that Zahner, and later Phil Murtaugh, saw the possibilities for a giant market in the future. After all, more than 65 percent of China's population still resided in rural areas. Incomes were limited. Farmers, traders, and small businessmen would be hungry for practical little runabouts with low prices. Mini vehicles would be to China what pickup trucks are to construction contractors in America—reliable workhorses.

Murtaugh persuaded his boss, Rudy Schlais, that investing in Wuling would be a good idea. But as former Shanghai GM executives recall, Rick Wagoner was reluctant, asking "Why should GM put money into such a small and un-remarkable company?"

If Shenyang in 1992 was "a place from where you could see the end of the earth," according to Jack Smith, then Liuzhou in 1997 may have qualified as the very end itself. Zahner recalled how in Liuzhou's primitive airport lounge he was squeezed into a tiny seat between one guy holding a giant birdcage and another guy with a chicken on his lap. "It was a different world from the ones I had known in Shanghai, Beijing, and Guangzhou."

People there needed a different kind of vehicle, too. By 2000, the market for these tiny box vehicles (the Chinese call them *mianbaoche* or "bread" cars because they are shaped like a loaf of bread) was close in size to the market for passenger cars.

The small, tough vehicles, powered by engines similar in size to what would be fitted to motorcycles in America, were ideal for China's smaller cities and towns and rural villages.

Owners could carry both people and goods between the city and the countryside. There was a narrow compartment up front for the driver and passenger. Only a few inches separated their noses from the windshield. The vehicle's back area offered the value. It could be used as an open-bed truck, or the owner could order a canopy top and make it a van. One could transport chickens and rice into town and then carry people back to the fields—making money both ways.

Traditionally, GM did not compete in the mini vehicle segment. But Murtaugh was not looking for a precedent inside GM. He was aiming to set new precedents in China.

Although the profits per vehicle were tight—sometimes as little as $100—the sales volumes could make things interesting in a hurry. Sell 50,000 vehicles and you take home five million dollars in profits. Sell five hundred thousand and the earnings would jump to fifty million. And that's before profits from parts and service.

In America, GM was routinely losing money on sales of small cars. "There's no profits in small cars," was the know-it-all GM (and Ford and Chrysler) refrain. In China, Wuling was making money on $5,000 trucks and buses. GM might be able to learn something for a change.

An openness to learning new things seemed to be a primary difference between the Chinese and their new American partners. "I really think, at some point, we [GM in America] stopped learning. We thought our success was guaranteed by what had been achieved in the past," said one former GM executive who had worked both in China and America.

Zahner left China in 2000 to lead the team pursuing acquisition of Daewoo. But his hopes of getting GM into the business of making small cars soon became a reality. David Chen and Frank Zhao traveled back to Wuling in January 2000 and hammered out a basic agreement within a month.

Once more, Murtaugh had to battle hard to win headquarters over to approve the investment. "But there's no money in small cars," they liked to remind Shanghai GM, as a professor would remind his slower students. The Detroit "experts" wanted to know how GM was ever going to make any money with these little runt vehicles.

Murtaugh and Hu Maoyuan at SAIC pushed ahead anyway. SAIC had invested first, taking a 51-percent share in 2001. GM joined in 2002 and secured a 34-percent share. Wuling Motors kept 15 percent. In June 2002, GM China, SAIC, and Wuling Motors announced the formation of SAIC-GM-Wuling Automobile Co. Ltd. in Liuzhou, Guangxi. The initial GM investment was less than $50 million.

The heart of any vehicle is its engine. This is even more true when the product is selling for just $5,000. The customer is also getting a steel frame, seats, windshield, and chassis, of course. But the key to the investment would have to be a reliable engine.

In 2004 Murtaugh, aiming to meet this crucial requirement, sent Thomas Rippon, global program manager of A/B Series Engines, to Liuzhou. (In the interim, GM had taken some time to assess how to help this new company really blossom. After making big profits in 2003, Shanghai GM could justify a major investment to improve the engine.) Rippon had supported the launch of the engine plant at Shanghai GM and had been working in China since 1998. He knew his way around.

Rippon quickly settled into the Li Jing Hotel, where the beds were hard as a rock. Sleeping on such a hard surface was tough for Rippon, a big, strong man with a reputation for blasting three-hundred-yard drives when the occasional golf outing came along. So he found a local company to make a four-inch-thick foam mattress topper and asked the hotel staff to make larger sheets to fit over the new, modified double mattress. That's the kind of improvising you have to do when living far from the comforts of Shanghai or Beijing.

There was one KFC and one McDonald's in town, Rippon recalled, but "no other western chains existed anywhere else in this city of one million-plus." LiQi, the local beer brand that ran just under a buck a bottle, became the favorite after-hours beverage of the GM engineers working on the project.

Rippon and a group of around fifty people got right to work on the number one priority: modernizing the engine and transmission. "While we wanted a quality product from Wuling, we didn't want to interfere with the low-cost mentality that continues to make this company a success. We [could] learn from them, avoiding waste and redundancy in our processes."

There were, in fact, three teams of people working to ramp up engine production. One was from SAIC-GM-Wuling (SGMW), one was from PATAC (an engineering and research joint venture formed by GM and SAIC back in 1997) and one from GM Daewoo Automotive Technology Co. Ltd. (GMDAT). Most were coming and going from Korea and Shanghai. Rippon and seven other contract engineers stayed in Liuzhou full time. The goal was to develop an engine plant capable of producing 350,000 engines per year.

Rippon led the SGMW team in taking charge of the engine design, sourcing, and local (made in China) parts-buying activities. Of key importance, the team of Koreans and Americans from GMDAT would maintain all of the intellectual property for the new family of engines under development. GM did not want a repeat of the Chery nightmare, so it was careful to keep all of the intellectual property in the hands of its Korean subsidiary where GM was the majority shareholder.

Rippon's team first developed 1.1 and 1.2 liter engines. In America, it was next to impossible to find any car on the road with an engine smaller than 2 liters, so 1.1 and 1.2 liter engines were considered real pipsqueaks. But Murtaugh and Rippon understood that these small engines were what people in the countryside could afford.

Rippon was halfway through his tenure in Liuzhou when Murtaugh resigned and Wale took over. SAIC-GM-Wuling in 2005 had already reached annual production of 310,000 micro trucks and vans, twice the number produced in 2002. Wale quickly grasped that there was going to be a need for more engine-making capacity.

The aim was to add a production facility in the northern part of China. A new engine plant, duplicating Rippon's plant in Liuzhou, was developed in Qingdao. Qingdao is a beautiful coastal city in Shandong province, one of China's agricultural breadbaskets.

It was best known for Qingdao Beer. The immediate target market for the mini vehicles made in Qingdao was found just beyond city limits, where ninety million Shandong province farmers and small businessmen made their home.

Once Qingdao got up to full production in the fall of 2007, SGMW was running two modern engine plants, each with capacity to make 350,000 engines per year. PATAC and SGMW cooperated to add 1.3 and 1.4 liter engines in Qingdao too. These would go into the company's most popular product, the Sunshine, a tiny, boxy minivan, shorter than a VW Beetle, designed to reliably transport five or six people over rural roads.

SGMW company website offers a description of the product's strong points: "Our Wuling Sunshine minivan has solid chassis, firm metal plate, increased interior space, and is of superior quality."

The new investments in capacity and higher-quality products paid off. By 2008, just three years later, sales at SAIC-GM-Wuling had doubled to 610,000 miniature vans and trucks per year. The new and improved Sunshine van accounted for 67 percent of sales. Thanks to careful control of product development costs, the profits per vehicle were expanding, too.

GM's formula for success was becoming clear: keep intellectual property in Korea at GMDAT, but take full advantage of low-cost manufacturing in China.

While Wale focused on increasing capacity at Wuling, Shanghai GM powered ahead on its own. The Chevrolet brand was positioned to appeal to the young, socially responsible new generation of Chinese car buyers. Many of those buyers would be found in the just-emerging inland city markets, away from the affluent coast.

Chevrolet products, positioning, and pricing were, by design, a notch below the more prestigious Buick. Chevrolet would retain an edge over similarly priced competitors like Hyundai or Nissan simply because of its image as an American product.

This was a remarkable feat of marketing when you consider that all the Chevrolet products built and sold in China were designed and engineered primarily in Korea. Chinese consumers—if they knew about the Korean origin—seemingly did not care. Chevrolet sales in China doubled to 203,000 between 2005 and 2008. Wale saw that China was "entering the vehicle acquisition stage and that demand was regionally dispersed," so it was mainly a question of "how quickly can you get the Chevy distribution network in place?"

Other major new milestones were achieved in rapid succession between 2006 and 2008:

- In 2006, GM China and SAIC formalized an agreement with the World Expo 2010 Shanghai Executive Committee to become the exclusive global automobile partner of World Expo 2010 Shanghai. Beijing would host the Olympic Games in 2008; Shanghai, ever competitive with the capital city, aimed to play host to a spectacular World Expo two years later.

- In October 2007, Shanghai GM signed a letter of intent with the People's Government in Anhui province to establish China's largest and most comprehensive vehicle proving ground.

- One month later, GM, SAIC, and Shanghai GM announced the establishment of a telematics joint venture called Shanghai OnStar Telematics Co. Ltd. China was home to the largest number of internet users of any country in the world, and many cars were fitted with navigational devices that displayed Chinese characters. GM's On-Star had already established a reputation for quality in America. The outlook in China was very promising.

- In the spring of 2008, GM, SAIC and Tsinghua University opened the China Automotive Energy Research Center (CAERC) in Beijing. CAERC was developing a comprehensive, integrated automotive energy strategy for China.

As of 2007, China was importing more than half of its oil, and leaders at the highest levels of power named energy security as a national priority. By teaming up with the "MIT of China," GM was securing a place to develop ideas and influence future policy, too.

There were many feel-good moments. Larry Zahner attended a GM top management meeting in Florida in 2007, where he met Shen Yang, the president of Wuling, whom he had not seen since their original encounter ten years earlier. Mr. Shen remembered that meeting well. He opened up his wallet and pulled out half of Zahner's business card. The two men laughed in delight.

In the spring of 2008, things were looking very good. Car sales were headed for another record year. GM had already ignited new activities in research, the proving grounds, and telematics services. GM had also secured the lead sponsorship position for the Shanghai World Expo. Chevy's dealer network was strong and sales were up. Wuling could not build mini vehicles fast enough to meet demand.

GMDAT was clearly crucial to the success of Shanghai GM. The company that was acquired for only $450 million in 2002 had become a key global manufacturing base for General Motors. The Buick Excelle, developed in Korea along with six other models, accounted for 70 percent of Shanghai GM sales in China.

"Without the GMDAT acquisition, Shanghai GM would not have had the success that it has had," confirmed a GM executive who had worked in China for more than four years. "The Buick Regal and the GL8 were very important to SGM's early success in China, but could not carry SGM into the future. The acquisition of Daewoo was a strong reason for the success of GM in China— and possibly for the globe."

In May 2008, as Wale marked his third anniversary as president of GM China, he had many reasons to feel not just relieved, but genuinely happy with the progress in China since his arrival—and optimistic about the future.

For Wale, the biggest challenge remained how to get an exact forecast of demand. Predicting the future, never easy, was about to get dramatically more difficult.

19

A CHILL WIND

Chinese consumers can behave like a school of fish when sensing the first sign of danger. They move together in tight formation in one direction and then, quite abruptly, shift direction and head somewhere else. Just like that.

Just like that, in the summer months of 2008, worry and fear put a distinct chill on the seemingly unstoppable China car market. Demand for cars began to slow a little in June. By September, the market had gone flat.

"I remember attending a client's dealer conference, and the management warned the whole network that 2009 would be slow and tough . . . the whole industry was prepared for a shutdown!" recalled Freda Wang, now a senior manager at Mercedes-Benz China Ltd.

The drag in car buying was not a question of running out of money. And there was no sudden credit crunch cutting off loans to new car buyers. More than 90 percent of purchases were still being made in cash. The decision to stop buying cars was driven by sentiment—feelings of fear and uncertainty.

The single most important influence in Chinese people's car-buying process is the opinion of family and friends. This is where Chinese culture has a powerful influence. When confidence is running high, people can decide to buy not for a specific need but simply because everyone else is getting a car.

Friends and family are apt to say: "Heavens, Li, everyone on the block has a new car—aren't you going to buy one?"

But the moment that sentiment turns negative, a different message takes over: "Heavens, Li, there's a money crisis in America, and it may be headed our way. Nobody in the neighborhood is buying a car. Why in the world would you be considering a car now?"

During the autumn of 2008, Chinese consumers were devouring news of the financial disaster befalling U.S. banks. They were transfixed by the catastrophic failures of the mighty American financial system. Most knew Bear Stearns and Lehman and Citibank only by their Chinese names. But that did not stop them from grasping the gravity of the failures, bankruptcies, layoffs, and credit freezes dragging down the American economy.

Like a dutiful school of fish, they did an about-face and began to tuck away their money. Including money for cars. Hearing about the downturn in the United States and huge number of lost jobs, Chinese people started to fear for their own jobs. Would American and other foreign companies in China cut back? Would there be layoffs? What would happen to China's thousands of export companies, so many of which had come to depend on the U.S. market for their success?

No one knew the answer. It was new territory for China and stunning for them to see America in such desperate straits. By the end of the year, the market had turned decidedly quiet. There was still overall year-on-year car market growth, but sales growth limped in at just 7 percent. That was the equivalent of a downturn for a market that had been recording better than 20-percent growth each year since 2000.

Shanghai GM took it on the chin, too. In 2008, the joint venture's sales reached 500,000 cars. That was an unhappy step backward from the 535,000 cars sold in 2007. For the first time in the history of Shanghai GM, the company did not grow at double digit rates. Quite the opposite: sales growth went into reverse.

There was more bad news. Sales of Buicks were down. Shanghai GM's key brand and generator of most of the firm's profits was on the defensive. Every Buick model—the Regal, the LaCrosse, the GL8 minivan, even the hugely popular Excelle—saw sales decline in 2008. Sure, Chevrolet was up. But the growth was tepid. Sales increased less than 5 percent, from 191,000 to 203,000 in 2007. Moreover, Chevy products earned far less in profit than Buicks.

GM put a brave face on the results. "Over the next two to three years, we will roll out five or more new products under both of our volume brands, Buick and Chevrolet," said Kevin Wale. "Our four other brands (Cadillac, Opel, Saab, and Wuling) will also bring out new and upgraded models to meet the rapidly changing needs of vehicle buyers nationwide."

It was true that the company was at the bottom of its product cycle and that new models were being readied for 2009. The all-new Buick Regal, a good-looking sedan, was launched in December. But there was no denying the widespread nervousness across the industry. Wale was quoted by the *China Daily* as saying GM expected the market in 2009 "to remain steady," which is corporate code for "flat" or "weak."

The U.S. car market was already reeling. It was on track to go from sixteen million units in 2007 to thirteen million in 2008 and then just ten million in 2009. Would China car sales drop like a stone too? Automakers in China scrambled in December 2008 to revise their production forecasts for 2009. Optimistic double-digit growth projections developed back in August were tossed aside. The industry consensus shifted to a projection of 5-percent growth in 2009—and even that seemed overly optimistic.

In late December, the Chinese government responded to the global financial crisis by announcing a stimulus package valued at $586 billion. China's economy was still growing at around 8 percent, according to official sources. But after witnessing the sudden economic carnage in the United States, the leaders in Beijing were taking no chances.

Predictably, Chinese consumers read that move as a vote of no confidence and slowed their spending even more. Restaurants in Shanghai and Beijing that had been jam-packed in August looked more empty than full in December. And car sales continued to stagnate.

Wale had said that one of the biggest challenges of working in China was getting an accurate forecast of demand. Now he was confronted with a market at a near-standstill. All of the investments in new plant capacity, the new proving grounds and research center that had looked so promising and timely only a few months earlier would be transformed into expensive cost centers if the market did not bounce back.

Times had changed, and many people had moved on. Chen Hong was no longer in charge at Shanghai GM. He had been named president of SAIC earlier in 2008, reporting to SAIC chairman Hu Maoyuan. Rick Swando was leading the GM efforts to crack the Russian market. Jack Smith and Rudy Schlais had retired a few years earlier. Phil Murtaugh was back in China, but now across the river as president and CEO of Chrysler Asia Pacific.

Shanghai GM had lost substantial ground in sales and in market share. After beating Volkswagen for three years in a row, Shanghai GM found itself behind both Volkswagen joint ventures in sales. Profits were not what they were supposed to be. In the space of just a few months, everything that had been steaming ahead suddenly slowed and then began to slide backward.

The City of Shanghai, owner of SAIC and half-owner of Shanghai GM, had never acquired a taste for going backward. This would not do.

20

THE FAVOR

Most Chinese no longer pay much attention to the writings of Chairman Mao. Even fewer foreigners take time to read his works. But that does not mean the Chairman has lost relevance. In fact, Mao still has much to offer those who want to come to grips with modern China.

"Who are our friends? Who are our enemies? This is the most important question . . ." That is the Chairman's opening sentence in Volume I of *The Selected Works of Mao Zedong*. There is a spectrum of friends and enemies that float in the back of the minds of most human beings. But in China, the cultivation and sorting of that spectrum is an art form. Chinese people—and companies— manage a sophisticated and active friendship spectrum. Sooner or later foreigners are bound to discover just where they fall on it.

There are six categories along the Chinese friend spectrum, ranging from distant (enemy/stranger) to very close (friend/family).

1. Enemy/Stranger (*Di Ren*)

   Anyone you do not know. An enemy and what westerners would call a stranger fit into the same category. They get the same treatment. Typical treatment of an enemy/stranger may well go something like this:

   It's a cold winter evening in Beijing. The streetlight changes and office workers step off the curb. An elderly woman in raggedy clothes—a beggar—approaches a young woman.

   "I'm hungry, I'm hungry . . ."

"You're hungry? I'm starving to death!" snaps the female executive as she holds her Gucci bag tighter and pushes by. She's not being cruel. In China's hypercompetitive society, there is often no time to care for strangers.

2. Friend (*Pengyou*)

   A friend is an acquaintance, someone you know by name but have no judgment about. The indifferent feeling rates barely a notch above what you feel for the stranger.

3. Old Friend (*Lao Pengyou*)

   A Chinese person can call you an "old friend" after knowing you for only a few months. Old friend usually means someone you see frequently but with whom there are no real meaningful ties. Calling you *lao pengyou* is just a little friendly gesture.

4. Good Friend (*Hao Pengyou*)

   This means some nonbinding ties have been established through a history of giving and taking. There are frequent exchanges of favors, but nothing is guaranteed.

5. Close Buddy (*Ge Mer*)

   The relationship is very close and approaches the status of a relative or family member. The same young executive who hurried past the beggar would spend her last dime and borrow more—she would do anything—to help out a *ge mer*.

6. Family/Relative (*Jia Ren*)

   When an immediate family member or a relative shows up at your doorstep, in trouble, the response will be immediate and comprehensive. Whatever is necessary will be done to help this person simply because the person is part of the family. It does not matter if you've never seen the person before. A third cousin from the other side of the country is still family.

The quickest and surest way to find out where you stand in China is to ask for a favor. When favors are done for friends, there is usually an expectation of receiving something in return.

At the start of 2009, neither Kevin Wale nor his boss Nick Reilly had any reason to even think about asking for favors. But by spring, getting help had become an urgent, if not publicly acknowledged, priority.

Overall, Wale's business was in good shape. So were GM operations across the Asia-Pacific region. Favors were required by many places inside GM as the events of 2009 unfolded—but not in Asia. Still, it was necessary to quell doubts for the Chinese press. "Our plants across China will operate normally," said Wale at a media briefing in Shanghai early in the year. "There will be no change in payments to employees, dealers, or suppliers contracted to GM China or to our joint ventures."

The one lingering risk Wale did not mention was products. Would Shanghai GM be able to count on a steady stream of cars from the GM's three key car development bases: the Buick division in America, GM's Opel subsidiary in Germany, and GMDAT in Korea? Detroit was in especially bad shape. As GM approached the end of the first quarter of 2009, things looked shaky for the North American operations and, by extension, the Buick brand.

Barack Obama was inaugurated as the forty-fourth president of the United States on January 20, 2009. He wasted no time in creating a special automotive task force to find ways to save General Motors, even if it meant running the firm through a speedy bankruptcy. The auto task force, led by Steven Rattner, wanted to reduce the number of GM brands to a small handful. Pontiac, Saturn, and Hummer were already on the block, primed for quick elimination. If not for its success in China, Buick would have certainly joined the group of brands on their way out the door.

That would be a problem for China. Buicks accounted for about 55 percent of Shanghai GM sales in China and an even higher share of its profits. The disappearance of Buick would have been a devastating blow to Shanghai GM. But Korea offered a backup: the Buick Excelle, which accounted for two-thirds of the Buick sales in China. The car was developed in Korea. And Korea was financially safe.

In the event that the Buick brand did get shuttered, the Excelle's brand identity in China could be migrated from Buick to Chevrolet. Shanghai GM had done the same thing previously when it switched the branding of the Sail from Buick to Chevrolet. Even if Buick were killed, Shanghai GM could still rely on GMDAT in Korea to supply 80 percent of its products.

In terms of supplying product to China, Opel, GM's subsidiary in Germany, was a worry too, but a smaller one. The brand-new Buick Regal, launched in December 2008, was designed and developed by Opel engineers. If Opel was sold or went bankrupt, then Shanghai GM would have to find a way to support the Regals already on the road in China with parts and service. And future production of the Buick Regal might be delayed or shut down entirely.

To be sure, North American and German operations were a financial mess. But GM's Korean operations were still running strong. GMDAT recorded its best year ever in 2008, selling in Korea and exporting some 1.9 million cars to more than a hundred markets worldwide. During the 2000s GMDAT improved on its special expertise in designing and developing small cars—and engines for those cars.

From its quiet base on the Korean peninsula, GMDAT was shipping cars and kits to Europe, the United States, Latin America, India, and, of course, China. In China, the car kits were married with parts made in China to make the Chevrolets and Buicks seen on the streets of Shanghai, Beijing, and other major cities. Chinese consumers loved the package: an American brand at an affordable price, with engines that sipped gas rather than guzzling it.

Shanghai GM was nicely insulated from the financial storms besieging the company in North America and Europe. Some in the industry talked about the possibility of GM Asia-Pacific going independent. Between Korea (with the design and development expertise) and China (with the manufacturing strength and enormous market), GM Asia-Pacific operations could not only stand on their own, but make nice profits too. "We're paying for their [GM] pensions back in America, and they don't even realize it," said one Chinese manager from Shanghai GM at the time.

By the end of the first quarter of 2009, standing on its own was no longer an option for GM in North America or in Europe. The same GM executives who for years did not really need assistance or ideas because "they had already thought about them" suddenly found themselves in the same position as the homeless woman on the Beijing street corner desperate for food. Except GM was desperate for money.

GM had advised shareholders in late 2008 that it would run out of cash in the first two quarters of 2009. "Volatility in the world's financial markets, tightening of consumer and business credit, and historically low consumer confidence has created a very challenging environment," said Rick Wagoner, GM's CEO and chairman.

After a review of the management team and the GM balance sheet, Steve Rattner, head of the team from Washington, recommended bankruptcy. It was the only way to clean up what was truly a disastrous balance sheet. He also wanted to fire Wagoner, who had been chairman and CEO of the company since 2000. Rattner told CBS News, "This is a company that could not tell you, on any given day, within five hundred million dollars, how much cash it had . . . not only were they not prepared, but Rick Wagoner had very specifically said he didn't want to prepare . . . frankly, it's an irresponsible position [for a CEO to take]." Rattner's sharp criticism of GM did not stop there: "The stunningly poor management that we found . . . among other things . . . perhaps the weakest finance operation any of us had ever seen in a major company."

Bailout-weary taxpayers were looking for someone, something to blame for America's economic nightmare, and Wagoner's was one of the first heads to roll. Wagoner announced his resignation on March 29, 2009. Forty days later, on May 7, GM announced its earnings for the first quarter. The company reported that revenues were down 44 percent and that it had lost another $6 billion.

"Our first quarter results underscore the importance of executing GM's revised Viability Plan, which goes further and faster to lower our break-even point," said Fritz Henderson, president and chief executive officer. "Our Plan is designed to fix the fundamentals of our business . . . This is a defining moment in the history of General Motors . . . Our goal is to fix this business once and for all to position ourselves to win in the long-term."

GM's "defining moment in history" was a bust: Less than thirty days later, GM was being escorted through bankruptcy. GM employees would never again hear talk of the Viability Plan to avoid bankruptcy.

Meanwhile, GM Europe had lost $2 billion during the first quarter. The Opel subsidiary was also in dire need of cash. There was talk of selling Opel outright to bidders from Canada and from a Russian-Belgian consortium. Even Italian automaker Fiat was in the hunt. If GM in America was dead, then Opel was at least critically wounded. It needed a cash infusion in a hurry. Opel submitted a viability plan to the German government, seeking $4.2 billion in European aid. Without the money, GM said, Opel could go out of business.

GM Asia-Pacific also suffered a loss in the first quarter. But the number was a mere $21 million, a drop in the ocean compared with the billions evaporating in America and Europe.

The only bright news for GM was that Chinese consumers had begun to recover confidence. In March, the Chinese government cut taxes on cars with small engines and offered subsidies to buyers of mini vehicles. The response was immediate and powerful. After languishing in the doldrums since the previous summer, China's car market started on a tear that would only build in strength through-out 2009.

At the beginning of the year, the consensus forecast for China's car market was for 5-percent growth. Each month the sales numbers increased. By the end of 2009, the market had rocketed to 8.3 million cars, from 5.8 million in 2008—an upward surge of 46 percent!

The pitiful condition of GM in North America and Europe in the first part of 2009 reminds us of a simple axiom in business: A company can run out of a lot of things and still survive. It can run out of stock. It can run out of technical people. It can run out of goodwill. It can run out of new ideas, at least for a while. But the one thing that a business absolutely, positively is not allowed to run out of is cash. When you run out of cash, it's over. No matter how good your product or how loyal your customer or how impressive your people, if the company cannot get its hands on cash or credit, then everything comes to a halt. Cash flow is everything.

So while GM North America and Europe were fighting for their lives, GM Asia-Pacific had managed to stay above the fray. Above the fray, that is, until a foreign exchange bet went badly, badly wrong.

In the spring of 2009, some quiet, urgent scrambling was taking place in Korea. GMDAT suddenly had a severe cash flow problem. Executives from GMDAT were asking creditors for more time. GMDAT chief executive officer Michael Grimaldi said that "GM Daewoo continues to operate as normal" but that the company was "still in need of securing emergency funding as its U.S. parents' troubles and the global economic slump put it into financial distress" according to a report published in the *Global Times*, a Chinese newspaper.

The situation was like a football team marching downfield in the final minutes of the Super Bowl. They may have terrific momentum. But if the clock runs out before they reach the end zone, they lose the game. They can plead with the officials to put time back on the clock, but it is probably not going to happen.

Yes, exports from GMDAT were down in the first quarter of 2009. But that was not the main cause of the crisis. No, there was a much bigger problem hidden from view. The team in charge of finances at GMDAT had made a bet. The bet, approved all the way up the chain of command to the GM CFO in Detroit, was that the Korean currency would strengthen against the U.S. dollar as the United States fell more deeply into its financial crisis.

But, as fate would have it, the Korean won went the other way. In fact, instead of appreciating, the Korean won weakened against the dollar by as much as 50 percent in the period from July 2008 to January 2009.

When you make the wrong call on foreign exchange, the results can be calamitous. By the end of the first quarter on 2009, GMDAT foreign exchange losses had soared to $1.5 billion! In normal economic conditions, GMDAT's foreign exchange trauma would have stung badly but would still have been manageable. The company would appeal to its parent or to its bank and ask for another loan. If that did not work, the company could approach its shareholders and suggest a recapitalization.

But the spring of 2009 was no normal time. It was the height of the world's greatest financial crisis in seventy years. Even the most highly respected companies struggled to get lines of credit at the bank. Large segments of the global financial system were still frozen.

Executives at GMDAT approached the shareholders—the Korean Development Bank (KDB), Suzuki Motor, and SAIC—with a recommendation for recapitalization. All minority shareholders, including SAIC, declined. The refusal by KDB was understandable. It wanted some loans paid off before any talk of injecting more money into the company. Suzuki had no strategic interest in GMDAT, and therefore no incentive to write a check.

SAIC's rejection, however, must have hurt. After all, weren't they good friends, even *ge mer*? GMDAT supplied Shanghai GM with 80 percent of the product kits that it turned into finished cars for Chinese consumers. If the Korean operation were to collapse, where would Shanghai GM get its cars?

SAIC had earlier suffered an embarrassing setback in Korea after it purchased a controlling stake in SsangYong Motor Company, a specialty Korean automaker. The investment did poorly from the start and ended in bankruptcy. Maybe SAIC was still stinging from that mistake? In any case, at this critical juncture the Chinese decided not to ante up fresh capital.

By May 2009, GMDAT, just like its parent company GM, was running out of cash. It asked the KDB for a billion-dollar loan on top of the $2 billion line of credit from KDB that had already been exhausted. KDB held fast. KDB and other banks in Korea said no to a new loan.

With great reluctance, however, KDB and other Korean banks agreed to roll over half of the outstanding loan payments. On April 29, Reuters reported that a lead Korean creditor had said: "South Korean banks will roll over expiration of half of $890 million in short-term foreign currency forwards of GM Daewoo, the South Korean unit of cash-strapped General Motors Corp."

GMDAT had managed to talk the referee into putting a little time back on the clock. With Korean operations now under enormous financial pressure, China stood out as the only healthy operation in GM's world. And demand for cars in China, contrary to everyone's predictions a few months earlier, began to accelerate like never before.

Government tax breaks announced in March not only had triggered strong demand for small vehicles, but also seemed to be a real confidence builder for buyers of all cars, small and large. The giant school of fish otherwise known as the Chinese consumers had once again switched directions, to SGM's great relief. By the end of the summer, China was well on its way to becoming the world's largest car market, surpassing the United States in the process. There was even talk about how GM might leverage China to get out of trouble.

In a *TIME* Magazine article on May 18, 2009, correspondent Bill Powell wrote:

> Rumors circulated that GM was in talks with Shanghai Automotive Industry Corp., China's largest carmaker, to reduce its stake in a key 50–50 joint venture—Shanghai GM—as a way to raise cash to send back to Detroit. Wale had to knock that talk down. "Absolutely untrue," he tells TIME—GM executives say none of their China operations are for sale. Reilly was informing everyone at the Shanghai Auto Show that, while the China unit obviously could not count on injections from Detroit, growth plans are "self-financing."

The financial situation at GM was clear: Shanghai GM was awash in money. GM units in America, Europe, and Korea were starving for cash. GM International had traditionally relied on lines of credit through the parent company to secure necessary funding. Now, with GM getting American taxpayer money, that banking channel was shut tight.

Throughout the summer, GMDAT appealed to KDB for more time, fresh loans, or both. KDB would hear none of it and was fast losing patience. At the end of September, when $100 million in GMDAT loans was about to come due, KDB went public with its frustration. KDB CEO Min Euoo-sung warned: "If General Motors does not play the role of the largest shareholder of GM Daewoo in an appropriate manner, we will start to retrieve loans that will mature this month."

KDB was preparing to collect loans from GMDAT, a company with no cash. That is banking language for taking something over or shutting it down.

The government of Korea had no appetite for helping out, either. Said Kim Young-sun, chairwoman of the governing Grand National Party National Policy Committee: "GM Daewoo's management is putting the company's future at stake instead of trying to rationally resolve the mess they made."

GMDAT needed a favor—desperately. By September 2009, the company had exhausted all possible resources for cash and had nowhere left to turn. The clock was ticking and time was running out. Then, just a few weeks later, came two surprise announcements in rapid succession:

First, GM declared that it had completely changed its mind about Opel. The company was no longer for sale. This was a stunning and bold about-face, given that all of the terms of sale to the Canadian parts firm Magna and a Russian investment bank Sberbank, had already been finalized after months of negotiation.

Germany's Chancellor Angela Merkel was incensed—her government had lent Opel more than $2 billion over the summer to keep it alive and preserve the jobs of the twenty-five thousand employees at Opel. She learned about the reversal only forty-eight hours after having met with President Obama in the White House. And a senior Russian diplomat poured scorn on the move, calling it a "peculiar American style of doing business."

Then, just two weeks later, in mid-November, GM revealed that it had managed to recapitalize GMDAT by injecting $491 million of fresh money into the company. GM's crucially important international operations in Europe and Korea had managed, in a matter of weeks, to go from the doghouse to the penthouse.

How could this have happened? How could GM have moved so suddenly and so decisively from weakness to apparent strength? They must have found a channel to money. They must have found a favor.

But where?

PART FIVE

THE END OF THE BEGINNING

21

A MEMORY PALACE

On December 5, 2009—less than six weeks after GM suddenly found money to recapitalize its Korean operations and take back its offer to sell Opel—the *Wall Street Journal* reported on a highly unusual event:

> **GM, SAIC Re-Shape Partnership**
>
> BEIJING—General Motors Co. announced plans Friday to cede control of its key Chinese joint venture to partner SAIC Motor Corp. SAIC's stake in Shanghai General Motors Corp. will rise to 51% from 50% at a time when China is overtaking the U.S. as the world's largest auto market, though GM described the move as a technicality. The Chinese group will have the right to approve budgets, strategy and senior management appointments.

This was startling news. No foreign car company had ever willingly given up control to its Chinese partner. Chinese and foreign shareholders had always clung tenaciously to their respective ownership in the joint ventures, each aiming for control, profits, and dividends. Whether the foreign company be Mercedes-Benz or Toyota or Hyundai or Peugeot, the 50-percent share of the joint venture had forever been paramount to holding ground in China.

In the same *Wall Street Journal* article, GM officials acknowledged that the company had "been able to achieve some funding for other activities [in China] from the Chinese banking sector, which would have been difficult to do on our own . . ."

Achieve some funding that would have been difficult to do on our own. Though details were never made public, GM Asia Pacific had somehow managed to secure loans from Chinese banks. As with all loans, there would be a need to repay the original principal—plus interest.

Thirty years earlier, Deng Xiaoping had launched China's reform and opening policy. It was a bold new direction for the country, much as GM's entry into China in the late 1990s marked a new and uncertain path for the company. His advice to "cross the river by first feeling for the stones"—words that every Chinese person knows—was a pragmatic reminder to watch your step.

General Motors had been negotiating the great, unpredictable river of China for twelve years, carefully feeling for stones one step at a time. And GM's vigilance and perseverance had paid off: Chinese consumers were placing orders for Buicks and Chevrolets faster than they could be built. GM's joint venture with Shanghai Auto Industry Corp. had sold eight hundred thousand vehicles in 2009. Profits approached one billion dollars. China had become GM's most lucrative division in the world.

Why then, at the height of its success, would the company give up control? Extraordinary financial pressures can force a hand. In the fall of 2009, GM had to take a new, unplanned step. This time, there was no time to feel for stones. A leap had to be taken—and taken now.

GM executives later passed off the share sale as "a favor to our Chinese partners," citing new Chinese regulations that allowed SAIC to consolidate joint venture earnings only if it had a controlling share. GM officials were quick to add that they had an option to buy the 1 percent back from SAIC at any time.

"Good luck getting *that* back," is how one GM executive who used to work in China commented on prospects for recovering the 1-percent equity at some date in the future.

If compliance with new financial reporting regulations was the real reason for the share sale, then why did other foreign joint ventures not sell shares and cede control, too?

GM's favor gave its Chinese partner 51-percent ownership in Shanghai GM. Overnight, GM relinquished control. The Chinese were now officially in charge of Shanghai GM, a company that by 2011 was on track to sell 1.1 million vehicles and earn estimated revenues of more than $17 billion, according to industry sources familiar with Shanghai GM operations. But GM China officials would not confirm these estimates. Even after its U.S. bankruptcy filing and government rescue, GM's culture still showed signs of friendly arrogance. How could a company that's 33-percent owned by the U.S. government not be prepared to talk about expected revenue at one of its most valuable operations in the world?

Some media channels reported that the value of the 1-percent equity sale was just $85 million—a very modest figure, given that annual revenues at Shanghai GM were approaching $20 billion. When asked to confirm the amount, GM China officials said: "We are not discussing in public how much SAIC paid." If this share sale was just a technicality, then why not disclose the purchase amount?

Maybe the share sale in December 2009 was a favor returned. Maybe GM felt obliged to give up the 1 percent because its Chinese partner had delivered a lifeline in the midst of a life-or-death financial crunch that autumn. Maybe GM felt so obliged that it would have given the share for just one dollar.

But Deng would have had a question for GM: *Did you feel for the stones before selling the share?*

There are intriguing parallels between foreign companies like GM in China today and the saga of a talented Jesuit priest named Matteo Ricci who came to China in the late sixteenth century.

Ricci's mission was to convert the Chinese to Christianity, much as GM works to convert Chinese car buyers to Buick ownership. Working from his initial perch in Macao, Ricci needed to find a way—a hook of sorts—to get China's attention. That leverage came in the form of an advanced method for remembering things, known as the *memory palace*. It was a magnificent system of recollection by association.

> He told [the Chinese] that the size of the palace would depend on how much they wanted to remember: the most ambitious

construction would consist of several hundred buildings of all shapes and sizes; "the more there are the better it will be," said Ricci, though he added that one did not have to build on a grandiose scale right away.

—Jonathan D. Spence,
The Memory Palace of Matteo Ricci

Memorization was extremely important to those ranking officials whose sons were preparing for the civil-service exams. Ricci was able to trade his useful "technology" of the day for access to Chinese leaders at the city and provincial levels. Over time, he developed relations with the most senior officials in China's political hierarchy.

Then, after a lifetime of exchanging his special know-how for "market access," Ricci became the first westerner allowed to enter the Forbidden City. He was appointed an official advisor to the emperor. Ricci was extremely hopeful—if he could just convert the emperor, then all of China would become Christian, too!

But Ricci's mission was not to be accomplished. He was never permitted an audience with the emperor. Ricci had been very useful to the Chinese—up to a point. But "what need did the emperor have for Catholicism when he himself was already the Son of Heaven?" came the rhetorical question from the emperor's protective eunuchs. A disheartened Ricci lived out his days in Beijing. He died of influenza at the age of fifty-eight and was buried there.

To this day, foreign companies are welcome in China so long as they are useful. GM has been very helpful to China and, together with SAIC, has built a business to be proud of. But it is impossible to forget that GM's partner, SAIC, has its own global ambitions.

For GM's wheels to keep some traction on Chinese roads, the American company must wield real leverage. Accepting a minority position in Shanghai GM joint venture brings GM one step closer to the day when it may be told there will be no audience with the emperor.

22

THE GREAT TIDE

While GM was fighting for its life in 2009, Li Shufu, founder of Geely Motors, put into motion a grand plan to acquire a European luxury automaker. In early 2010, Geely closed the deal on the acquisition of Volvo Cars, the Swedish carmaker, from Ford Motor Company for $1.8 billion.

Li's vision was to produce two hundred thousand Volvo luxury cars a year in China, which would mean doubling Volvo's global production. Few analysts believed that number would be attainable in the foreseeable future. But even fewer observers ever thought they would see the day when Geely, a company from the Chinese countryside, would buy a globally renowned brand like Volvo.

It was seven years earlier, in 2003, that Li hosted a foreign visitor, an investment analyst, at his assembly plant in rural Taizhou, Zhejiang Province. At that time, Geely was still a very small player, making just a hundred thousand cars a year. Li and his guest ate lunch at a small wooden table in a private room adjacent to the workers' canteen, at the edge of the company's gravel parking lot. There was rice and some simple smaller dishes—fish, beans, and soup. The men sipped jasmine tea. The thirty-nine-year-old Li was pressing his paper napkin in tight hard rotations on the dining table with one hand and taking calls on his Nokia cell with the other. He spoke Mandarin to a Beijing official on one call, then reverted to his native Taizhou dialect on the next. His long hair sweeping down across his forehead made him look more like an artist or a writer than a street-smart businessman from Taizhou. Li paused and looked over at his guest:

"You like a beer?" he asked in Chinese.

"No, thank you," said his visitor.

Li appeared a little disappointed and said: "A car needs gasoline, and a man needs to drink!" *Che xuyao you, ren xuyao jiu!*

An hour earlier, the two men had sat side by side in a giant meeting room with high ceilings in the main building of the Geely headquarters. There were enough seats around the perimeter of the room to hold fifty people. Large windows at one end looked out on the Tiantai Mountains in the distance. A full plate of fruit sat on a small wooden table between them. Li slid back on his red overstuffed chair, complete with white doily draped over the back, and talked as if speaking to an entire room of people, not just the sole visitor to his right.

"My business plan is very simple, you see: We here at Geely will make affordable cars for the masses." That's what Chinese do. Manufacture at low cost. There is no sense in standing in the way of this great tide of history, he explained. China is the place to make cars, now and for decades to come.

"It's like planting trees," Li explained, leaning forward now to thrust his arm toward the ground. "The company will plant seedlings all over the [poorer] inland cities first, then later come into the [richer] coastal cities."

When the visitor remarked that the plan sounded much like Chairman Mao's revolutionary strategy of taking the countryside and then invading the cities, Li responded with an extended "Eeehhhh!" This is a Chinese way of letting you know that you've gotten the point, precisely.

Geely, like Chery, was never part of China's master automotive plan. Also like Chery, it never formed a joint venture with a foreign company. Li didn't believe in it. *A joint venture—what for? Is making a car so complicated that I can't do it myself?* "A car is just four wheels, a few sofas, plus a lid and an engine." Li, an entrepreneur's entrepreneur, exuded tremendous confidence: "From now on, selling cars will be just like selling watermelons."

"No sense in fighting the tide of history," he advised his visitor again. "Manufacturing is here in China. The best thing American companies can do is bring their brands over here; we'll do the production and then stick their brands right on the finished product." Li pantomimed applying a sticker to a new product.

China has never made a secret of its automotive industrial strategy: partner up with foreign companies, absorb the technology, and then make cars on its own. Li had instead decided to bypass the joint venture strategy and go straight for an acquisition. In 2010, Li got his brand—Volvo.

However, in the twenty-seven years since Beijing Jeep was formed, Chinese brands have managed to win only 30 percent of the domestic passenger-car market. Ironically, three independent companies outside of the central government's plan—Chery, Geely, and BYD—account for most of the Chinese share.

Conversely, major state enterprises that have partnered with off-shore builders in joint ventures—like SAIC, First Auto Works, Beijing Automotive, Dongfeng Motors, and Guangzhou—manage to take only small slivers of the market with their own brands. Their real growth comes through their joint ventures with foreign companies.

This has been a point of some embarrassment for the big state enterprises, which were selected to lead China's charge into auto manufacturing more than two decades ago. By this point, these organizations were supposed to be building cars that China could call its own, not watching the likes of Geely and Chery and BYD steal the lead.

The execution of China's national car strategy has been slow for two reasons. First, the plan assumed that the Chinese state enterprise partners in the joint ventures would be very aggressive about acquiring the technology from their foreign guests. But most Chinese partners have been co-opted by making large profits from building and selling already-designed cars from Japan, America, Korea, and Europe.

It makes sense. When you're a senior executive of a state enterprise, why insist on a new Chinese product when you can make handsome profits simply through manufacture and distribution of cars developed by your partner?

At Beijing Jeep, there was an initial insistence by the Chinese side to make a Chinese product. In fact, the negotiations dragged on for more than four years, until American Motors finally agreed that the joint venture would start out by designing and developing a brand-new Chinese Jeep for the China market. But Beijing Jeep was less than six months old when executives from American Motors persuaded their partners to totally drop the idea of an all-new product. Instead, they explained, the joint venture could make money right away by assembling Jeep Cherokees with parts imported from America.

And so it went. "Once they saw the money coming in and their salaries increasing," recalls Lauren Giglio, former Beijing Jeep director of finance, "they forgot all about developing a new Chinese product."

A second reason is that the foreign companies are very interested in keeping the technology to themselves. Their strategy is to forestall the creation of a future Chinese competitor for as long as possible.

Into this combative arena stepped Jack Smith in 1997 with a revolutionary new approach. "Whatever they need, we give it to them"—that's what several senior GM executives recall Smith saying when the Shanghai GM venture was formed. Smith was making a bold gamble that by demonstrating GM's largesse with know-how, the Chinese partners at SAIC would reciprocate by redoubling their own efforts to make the joint venture a success. No other foreign car company in China—before or since—has dared to take such an open approach.

GM's generosity with know-how places Shanghai GM in a unique position among joint ventures in China today. The 51-percent Chinese, 49-percent American joint venture is now able to develop new cars independently. "One of the reasons the joint venture has been so successful is that GM really responded to the needs of SAIC," said Janet Weatherbe, vice president of General Motors Asia-Pacific Operations from 2004 to 2007. "When you give, you get. The sharing made both companies stronger."

Proof of this came in January 2010 when Shanghai GM launched production of the Chevrolet New Sail. Priced at around $9000, the New Sail was designed and engineered inside China by engineers at Shanghai GM together with engineers from PATAC, the SAIC-GM joint venture engineering center set up in 1997.

The intellectual property for the vehicle belongs to Shanghai GM and PATAC, not GM. Today, there are around 1,900 engineers working at PATAC, nearly double the number in 2006. Also unlike previous Shanghai GM products, there is no royalty paid by Shanghai GM to General Motors for the Sail. Shanghai GM designs, engineers, manufactures, assembles, and distributes the New Sail. It pays GM only to license use of the Chevrolet brand.

The New Sail breaks into unprecedented territory on intellectual property ownership and exports. In a way, Shanghai GM is just what the Chinese government has wanted all along: a company with the ability to design and develop its own car, secure rights to the intellectual property, export, and, of course, have a controlling interest in the company. The only piece of the puzzle that's missing is the brand, Chevrolet, which they can and do license from GM.

The intellectual property for other products made by Shanghai GM still belongs to GM. But the New Sail would seem to indicate a trend, a direction remarkably similar to the one envisioned by Chairman Li back in 2003 when he talked about not standing in the way of the great tide of history.

In 2010, more than one hundred and thirty thousand Chinese consumers placed orders for the New Sail. Like its predecessor, it is a four-door compact car that is aimed at first-time car buyers in China's second- and third-tier cities. With fuel efficiency as one of the car's main selling points, the cars are powered by 1.2 liter and 1.4 liter S-TEC engines. These high-efficiency engines allow drivers to travel a hundred kilometers on as little as 5.7 liters of gas.

"SAIC and GM are great partners, where PATAC can tap into GM global engineering and GM's hundred years of knowledge and experience and best practices from around the world, while SAIC provides tremendous understanding of the local market and local resources," says Maryann Combs, president of PATAC. "PATAC has achieved vehicle and power train [engine and transmission] development capability. That includes design, development, and testing services."

For years, Chinese partners in joint ventures have been negotiating hard for the rights to export products from China. As a rule, the foreign car partners have blocked exports, because shipping cars from China would mean having to share revenue and profits with their Chinese partners. Better to ship from their home market and keep all of the money.

When they absolutely could not block exports, they shipped modest numbers of products to small markets. In the 1990s, Chrysler channeled exports of Chinese-made Jeep Cherokees to Burma and Cambodia. Volkswagen also sent small batches of Santanas to Vietnam and Laos. One Chrysler executive who worked at Beijing Jeep recalled, "At times we [at Chrysler] thought about just dumping them in the Pacific" to avoid the hassle and risks of selling old Chinese-made models into new markets.

And so another important milestone was passed when Shanghai GM began exporting the Chevrolet New Sail to Chile in October, 2010. The first export order was for nearly ten thousand cars, and plans are in place to sell the small family sedan to additional markets in South America, North Africa, and the Middle East.

These are remarkable developments: more products, higher sales, increasing exports, and surging profits. But who is now in control of the Shanghai GM joint venture? When the inevitable differences of opinion arise, who has the final word? For how much longer will it be true for GM that "when you give, you get"?

"Eventually they want to get it down to just one ISP—the controller—to watch where the money goes," half-joked a veteran employee who had worked at Shanghai GM for five years. ISP stands for *international service personnel*, a GM corporate label for the expert men and women who have transferred their know-how to Shanghai GM since 1997. ISPs tend to be very good at their jobs but are also very expensive to employ in China. These days, there are fewer and fewer GM ISPs in China.

Kerry Ivan of Beijing Jeep was an ISP back in the 1980s. He made $100,000 per year plus benefits, while his Chinese counterpart took home less than $5,000 annually. By the late 2000s, the salary gap had narrowed considerably, but the costs beyond the paycheck— that is, benefits—were another story. And these benefits are extraordinarily far-reaching.

In Shanghai, tuition at the elementary school level is in the range of $10,000 per year. For high school, tuition goes up to $15,000. Tuition for ISPs' children is covered by the company. Housing in Shanghai is surprisingly expensive, too. Most ISPs live in accommodations that run $8,000 to $12,000 per month. That's more than $100,000 per year just for housing.

Often, foreign companies also provide a car and a driver. In the event of a car accident in Shanghai, people bargain and settle right there on the spot. Drivers get out of their cars, do a careful walk-around, and then start raising their voices at each other. One side is going to transfer some money to the other side, and the high-pitched shouting is all about determining fair market compensation for the damages.

Rather than risk that the ISPs might run into an exceptionally aggressive (or clever) Chinese bargainer, the company normally provides a driver. That can cost between $500 and $800 per month, not including overtime pay.

There is a reason for the high costs. For all of its spectacular growth, China can still be a distressing place to live. The air pollution, even in progressive Shanghai, renders the sky a filmy, dusty brown on many days.

Driving is dangerous, too. More than 90,000 people were killed on Chinese roads in 2009, compared to around 33,800 in the United States.

Then there are disturbing incidents, like the baby milk powder scandal in 2008 when some Chinese companies adulterated the milk powder with melamine. More than thirteen thousand babies across China were sickened by the milk powder, hundreds were hospitalized, and six died of kidney stones or kidney failure. The director of China's Administration of Quality Supervision, Inspection and Quarantine (AQSIQ) was forced to resign as a result.

Living in China puts a lot of pressure on spouses, too, most of whom do not speak Chinese. Shanghai housing features thin insulation. As a result, homes tend to be unevenly heated. Spouses staying at home can find themselves spending long stretches of time huddling next to space heaters just to avoid the deep Shanghai chill. Families often need to wear three or four layers of clothing inside the house.

Many families hire Chinese maids for around $300 per month to do the housework. But the difference in culture and language ironically produces more anxiety than help.

- That brand new $120 Salvatore Ferragamo tie? It's hanging on the line to dry, damp and slightly crumpled, right next to the socks.

- Your kid's favorite blankie? You motioned to the maid to put it in the next room. She understands something else. And the next day you find out that it's been taken away with yesterday's trash.

- You can step out of your house for five minutes and return to find that all the doors have been locked and the maid has gone to lunch. She's terrified that something in the house might go missing. So you're locked out.

Take a family with two kids in school. The expenses for one year—not including the salary—can easily reach $200,000. Add the salary and other expenses and the average cost quickly climbs above $400,000. ISPs need to feel comfortable in order to perform well at their jobs. Comfort is very expensive in China.

"In the early 2000s, the cost of having 100 ISPs at Shanghai GM was the same as the 1,000 Chinese employees," said a senior executive at Shanghai GM. It was not the salaries that made the difference—it was the overall cost. Naturally, the issue of ISPs working at Shanghai GM was very important to the shareholders, GM and SAIC.

ISPs were at Shanghai GM to develop and install world-class processes that would stay with the joint venture long after the ISPs had gone home. The Chinese shareholders were very happy to get help, but they felt anxious when they saw the cost of ISPs. "How many cars will the joint venture need to sell just to pay for the ISPs?" they would ask aloud.

So an annual tug-of-war occurred at every car joint venture when it came to determining the right number of "imported experts." Shanghai GM was no different. The negotiations were like a human resource version of Beijing Jeep's earlier battles over the car's "kit price." From the Chinese point of view, there was only one way to make profits and stay competitive. In time, the kit price should go down. And accordingly, in time, the number of ISPs should go down.

More and more talented Chinese who had studied and worked in America were now returning to find jobs in China. Chinese could do the same jobs as the ISPs—at far lower cost.

As China's car market exploded, the number of people working at Shanghai GM naturally escalated, too. In 2010, Shanghai GM had ten thousand employees, up from fewer than a thousand a decade earlier. The total number of ISP employees, on the other hand, fell from one hundred to just forty-five. ISPs were now less than half a percent of the total Shanghai GM workforce. "It's getting more arm's-length—I guess GM's gonna try to run [the joint venture] from the outside," said a manager at Shanghai GM.

The dwindling number of ISPs—GM experts—is a powerful indicator of just how self-sufficient Shanghai GM has become. Chairman Li's 2003 prediction about manufacturing and the "great tide of history" continues to look highly prescient.

Where will that tide take China's auto industry—and GM—in the future?

23

ELECTRIC CARS
AND ELEVATORS

Chinese consumers bought seventeen million cars, trucks, and buses in 2010, thus making China home to the largest vehicle market in the world, easily surpassing the United States. And the Chinese rush to cars is only getting started: 90 percent of cars are bought with cash. Ownership penetration levels are low—there are just 45 million cars on the road in China, compared with 240 million in the United States. If you take 2010 car sales in the other BRIC countries—Brazil, Russia, and India—and double them, the China market is still larger and growing faster.

Phenomenal numbers like these create euphoria among carmakers, dealers, parts suppliers, customers—everyone, it seems, except the leaders in Beijing in charge of national security. They worry about how to supply Chinese motorists with enough gasoline.

More than half of China's oil comes from overseas. Chinese leaders want to take action before China, like America, becomes addicted to oil. Their answer is to go electric. The vision, first outlined in late 2008, is to make China the world's leading producer and consumer of electric vehicles.

Embracing electric cars offers China a huge benefit beyond weaning the nation off of oil: if China could lead in electric cars, then Chinese automakers would have a way of leapfrogging the foreign car makers in technology. Instead of playing catch-up in the field of traditional gasoline and diesel engines, China could burst ahead through innovation in battery-powered cars.

The central government has declared a commitment to making China a leader in electric vehicles. Officials in Beijing have identified twenty cities nationwide to serve as the incubator markets for electric vehicles. SAIC once invited GM and Ford to bid for a "luxury sedan" joint venture to rid China of its overdependence on imported cars. Now China has invited foreign companies to participate in its newest great leap—electrics.

In 2010, six of the twenty Chinese cities qualified for subsidies of up to 60,000 RMB ($8,900) for the purchasers of clean-energy vehicles. The target is to produce one million electric vehicle sales annually by 2020. It is not uncommon for the Chinese authorities to make such bold declarations, even when they are at odds with reality. It's an accepted way of lending weight, if not credence, to their designs. China has far to go to meet those lofty goals. In 2009, sales of hybrids and electric vehicles in China came to only a thousand cars. (As of this writing, GM planned to introduce its Volt to China in early 2011.)

Yet the mere promise of a breakthrough by China in electric vehicles was strong enough to stoke enthusiasm among private equity investors, carmakers, and academics. "If I were a betting man," declared Dan Sperling, member of the California Air Resources Board and professor at UC Davis, "I would say that electric vehicles have the best prospects for success right here in China." Professor Sperling was the keynote speaker at the first annual US-China Electric Vehicles Forum in Beijing in September 2009.

Warren Buffett—one of the world's most intelligent investors— seems enthusiastic too. In September 2008, a subsidiary of Buffett's Berkshire Hathaway invested $230 million for a 9.9-percent share in BYD, a young Chinese car company based in Shenzhen, just north of Hong Kong.

BYD was already the world's leader in manufacturing batteries for cell phones. Its brilliant leader, the forty-four-year-old Wang Chuanfu, had decided only a few years earlier that BYD would enter the car business too. Wang's vision was to leverage battery technology to build battery-electric cars. He ignored fellow members of his board of directors who felt intimidated by the challenge, which was admittedly daunting: BYD had no experience in cars, and the China market was already flooded with more than fifty different brands.

Berkshire Hathaway's investment in late 2008 triggered a year-long buying spree by money managers in New York, London, and Hong Kong that catapulted the BYD stock from less than $10 a share in 2008 to more than $70 in early 2010. Investors made the connections among BYD's dominance in batteries, China's rise as the world's largest car market, and the government's ambition to make China a leader in electric cars.

Just like that, Chairman Wang became China's richest man.

In early 2010, BYD announced plans to begin selling its E6 electric-powered sedan in Los Angeles by the end of the year. Shares climbed even higher. But then there were delays and obfuscations. Pretty soon it was apparent that BYD would not be selling cars in Los Angeles as planned, at least not in 2010.

By the fourth quarter of 2010, BYD's stock had fallen back to around $45 per share. Investors were having second thoughts after BYD delayed launches of both its hybrid and electric vehicles. BYD had been making cars for less than six years. And those were small cars powered by ordinary gasoline engines—not batteries. The engines themselves were from a Mitsubishi engine plant in China!

Initially, investors had found BYD's story irresistible. Imagine the upside if BYD were to get it right! But after so many delays, the same investors began wondering whether BYD really had the ability to apply its expertise in cell phone batteries to the complex business of powering cars in a safe and reliable way. Investors were asking the same sort of questions of BYD as the British delegates had asked fifteen years earlier while waiting for the elusive Chinese minister to appear at the Beijing Auto Show:

> Question: Does BYD really have the technology to make competitive and reliable battery-powered cars?
>
> Answer: BYD does not say that they do not have the technology.

BYD remained unflappable despite the repeated delays of the promised electric cars. At a conference with analysts and the media in the fall of 2010, BYD chairman Wang indicated plans to extend his empire to the home appliance business.

"What next? I heard that you're going to make rice cookers, too," one analyst commented derisively.

Chairman Wang ignored the remark and turned his attention back to the prospects for electric cars. He talked about how BYD already had some e6 models in the Shenzhen city taxi fleet. Then he asked his listeners to imagine the day when BYD E6 electric cars dominated the Shenzhen taxi fleet. Then he asked them to imagine all the other tens of thousands of taxis running in Chinese cities.

"Just think of the potential!" he said with some bravado.

Foreign companies are definitely thinking about the potential. On December 6, 2010, *Automotive News* published a story on the escalating interest in China's electric car market.

> Speaking in early November at an electrified vehicle symposium in Shenzhen, Tsinghua University professor Ouyang Minggao said that for China to reach its targets for electric vehicles, "we need international cooperation." Ouyang leads government-funded new energy vehicle projects.
>
> Many foreign battery companies are already working with Chinese automakers. Among them: A123 Systems Inc. of Massachusetts and SAIC Motor Corp. produce lithium batteries; Ener1 Inc. subsidiary EnerDel and China's Wanxiang EV Co. Ltd. will produce battery cells; and Johnson Controls-Saft supplies batteries to Chery Automobile Co.
>
> All are betting that China's EV sector will be big. They aren't alone.

While placing their bets, companies must never forget that to be dealt a hand in the game of electric cars—or almost any business in China—you will need to get approval for a license.

And get a partner.

Once those are secured, you will begin to compete with both the house and the player. The ones making the rules are also playing the game—and they're determined to triumph.

It's autumn 2010, on the sort of warm autumn Saturday afternoon in Shanghai that pricks the skin. Just as the heavy humidity settles on the back of your neck, Kevin Wale pulls up at Starbucks in a spotless Buick Enclave, greets his guest, and orders an icy Frappuccino. Looking cool and fresh, he has just an hour to talk between the GM China Family Day event that he just left and his next appointment.

Wale is president of GM China Operations, so the buck stops with him when it comes to GM's 49-percent shareholding in Shanghai GM. On this day, business is good. Very good. Shanghai GM is on its way to sales of one million vehicles for the year—an astonishing 35-percent increase over 2009. SGMW, the mini vehicle maker, will also top one million units in 2010, continuing its own meteoric ascent.

At more than two million units, Shanghai GM and SGMW now account for more than one quarter of GM's global sales. The money is good, too. Since the beginning of 2010, Shanghai GM has been contributing 30 percent of GM's worldwide profits.

The factories are humming. At the Shanghai GM plant in Pudong, they are running two ten-and-a-half-hour shifts every day, manned by three crews. "When the Chinese decide to do something, it's going to happen. It's like a force of nature," says Kenneth Molloy, executive director of quality at Shanghai GM.

Productivity is competitive with that of the rest of the world's carmakers. Of the six plants in the world that qualify for the "best lean production" practices inside GM, four are located in China.

General Motors is finally looking up, globally. The company has reported two successive quarters of profits and is scheduled to release more good news about the third quarter. Investment banks are in the midst of frenzied planning for an initial public offering for GM in November, when the U.S. government will sell its shares to the public. The goal of the Obama Administration is to recoup some of the $50 billion dollars that U.S. taxpayers injected into GM back in the spring of 2009.

Fifteen minutes into the conversation, the fifty-six-year-old Wale removes the plastic cap on his Frappuccino and starts working the ice chips at the bottom of his drink with the straw. His gaze remains fixed on the bottom of his cup as he talks about the business in China. "Relationships come first, second, and third, then business," Wale says. There are four board meetings a year, and he meets with his partners at SAIC often, carefully cultivating the relationship.

The biggest challenge for Wale remains nailing an accurate forecast of just how big and how fast the China market will grow. He has just come from a major conference in the Western city of Chengdu. Chinese auto industry leaders there were projecting vehicle sales of between twenty and twenty-five million per year by 2020. Others pushed even higher, predicting a level of thirty million within ten years.

In 2010, total demand for the Chinese auto market was already on track to top seventeen million units. Twenty million looks inevitable. Thirty million appears to be only a matter of time. "We try to stay a half or a full plant ahead," Wales says, referring to the planning required to build new factories early enough to stay in line with the growth.

Everything happens more quickly in China. "New models are introduced quicker, new plants go up quicker, and there is not always time for a structured approach," Wale says. China's frenetic pace forces Wale to respond to shifting conditions at all times and to make plans on the run. After a quick glance at the time, he sets down his cup, indicating that it is time to move on to his next appointment.

In early 2010, General Motors China moved into a shiny new high-rise office building. Previously, the employees had been scattered in separate offices in Shanghai's Lu Jiazui area, Pudong's "downtown." Now they were under one roof on Jinwan Road in the Jinqiao section of Pudong, a remote, lightly populated area with scattered warehouses, assembly plants, and office buildings.

They call the new building and adjacent field the GM China campus; it looks and feels like a suburban American office-building complex. "The air-conditioning system is very modern and energy efficient," the Chinese company official explains in English, further emphasizing the American influence here. The hallways are spacious and brightly lit. The people speak in hushed, polite tones. There is a large canteen on the ground floor as well as a convenience store, a room for ping-pong, and an internet area for visitors.

The eight hundred employees at GM China work in modern comfort in the relaxed and friendly atmosphere of the campus setting. The GM China building includes many amenities "on campus" because the nearest food and entertainment options are, inconveniently, more than a mile away. "Quite a few people complain about being stuck out there, away from everything. But the building is very nice," said a manager from a supplier company who has friends who work at the GM China campus.

A few miles away, many of the ten thousand employees of the Shanghai GM joint venture work in a seven-year-old office building in the same city. It may be the same city, but it is a different world. They are on the front lines, where battles for market share and profits are waged every single day. There is an energy in the bustling corridors that feels both invigorating and stressful. Chinese is the official language. Many of the employees have the drawn look that comes from late hours in the office and too many marathon meetings. The men and women of this facility may not look fresh, but their minds are still running at full speed. They have to. It's called survival.

Finished with his business for the day, a foreign visitor gets on the elevator at the top floor along with a couple of employees. The compartment stops at several more floors, and many people get on. Halfway to the ground floor, the elevator is jammed with people. There is no more room inside. Bodies are wedged in, with hips and shoulders and elbows touching here and there.

The elevator doors open on the next floor. A heavy-set young Chinese man in a suit and a buzz cut surveys the scene. The elevator is full. But rather than wait for the next elevator, he turns on his heel so that his back is toward the people inside. Then he begins to step backward into the elevator. His elbows are slightly protruded to make room on the left and the right as he presses in. No one says a word. He struggles but finally manages to get his entire body inside the compartment. Then he plants his feet.

Immediately the elevator begins to buzz. There is too much weight. It is unsafe and the doors will not close. *Brrng, brrng, brrng* go the warnings from the elevator. Someone needs to get off.

The big man in front does not move. He does not speak. He does not look to his left or right. He pushes his glasses up on his nose, crosses his arms, and stands still.

More *brnng, brngg, brnng* from the elevator, and no one says a word. Finally, after many, many seconds, there is movement at the back. The visitor signals his impatience with the situation. It's too hot inside the compartment. He wants out.

The big man in front moves slightly to the side, just enough to let the visitor step off. The alarm stops. Then he reaches over and quickly punches the Close Doors button, and the doors shut. The elevator is on its way again, full of people accustomed to tight quarters, annoying noises, and the stuffy air that comes with too many people crammed together and jostling for advantage every minute of the day.

That is how things are won and lost everywhere in China: a determination to occupy a space and hold onto it, no matter how uncomfortable. From ownership shares of a joint venture to space in an elevator, the Chinese way is take control and then press the advantage.

It remains arduous and hard to create a business in China, and it is still a long way to go to scale new heights.

Conclusion

THE END OF THE BEGINNING

If we think of competition in China's car market as a nine-inning baseball game, then GM is now playing the third inning. It is early, but what does the scoreboard say? And how will the company perform in the innings to come?

By just about every conventional business measurement—sales, growth rates, market share, profits—GM has been tremendously successful in China. Achievements that went far beyond expectations came as a result of hard work, resilience, and a willingness to adjust to fast-changing conditions.

Yet it is only when we understand the singular characteristics of China itself, and the forces at work in its dealings with foreign partners, that we can make a realistic assessment of GM's likely road ahead.

Chinese society today is driven by a modern trinity: work, money, and power. Work is absolutely necessary to accumulate money in order to enhance one's leverage. Taking it easy is not an option: the hefty fellow who forces himself into the packed elevator is not going to yield territory—it will be the smaller or less tenacious guy who loses ground.

Even the wealthy Chinese are driven. Wang Chuanfu, BYD's billionaire founder, was asked in 2010 about his work-life balance. He waved off the idea, explaining that Chinese people in his generation have no such concept.

Of course, foreign companies like GM are driven too, scouring the globe for growth and profits. The Chinese understand that the promise of money serves as a powerful magnet.

China's strategic enrichment formula looks like this:

1. Invite foreign investors.
2. Share some profits with foreign companies, but maintain tight controls.
3. Keep the money inside China.

In the first ten years of this century, China has lured in and then channeled *hundreds of billions* of foreign investment dollars into construction of tens of thousands of factories, stretching for miles on end across the country.

GM also built many factories in China. Its sales in China went from fewer than 100,000 cars a year in 2002 to more than 2.3 million in 2010. Countless other industrial plants now make every kind of product for China and for the world. Revenues from exports of everything from Nike golf clubs to iPhones to Christmas tree ornaments have helped China amass a foreign exchange fortune.

As of the end of 2010, the Bank of China was sitting on more than $2,800,000,000,000 in foreign reserves. Yes, that's almost three trillion dollars. By comparison, foreign reserves in export powerhouse Germany are $217 billion and the United States holds $135 billion.

China's aggressively mercantilist formula has worked incredibly well. Incomes are way up, infrastructure is vastly improved, and, most important, global production of a dazzling number of products is now planted firmly on Chinese soil.

What does all of this accumulated wealth mean for GM? China's careful cornering of money has led directly to the greatest car boom the world has ever seen. GM arrived in China at exactly the right time—Chinese people who could hardly afford a bicycle in the 1990s are today laying claim to Buicks faster than they can be built.

Partnering with China's most powerful city has played a large role in GM's success, too. Shanghai GM sold more than one million cars in 2010. But that success was not unique. The City of Shanghai's other car joint venture, Shanghai VW, also achieved sales of more than one million cars in 2010.

There are also some intangibles working in GM's favor. Chinese consumers seem to admire America. Or at least they admire the power that America projects. What they really care about are the American names—Buick, Chevrolet, Cadillac—and the prestige those names carry in today's China.

Of course, GM has done much, much more than just show up and benefit from an American halo effect. Shanghai GM was able to build a thriving business because the company evolved far away from the heavy-handed bureaucracies of GM headquarters in Detroit and planning officials in Beijing. If GM's headquarters had been in charge of Shanghai GM from the start, there is a good chance that, like so many of GM's other overseas ventures, it never would have gotten off the ground.

Winning customers and earning record profits, however, has not lead to any obvious accrual of power and traction. On the contrary: GM and other foreign companies find that in exchange for growth and profits they must surrender control on some crucial fronts. Foreign companies in China feel like they are playing a permanent away game.

In March 2011, the American Chamber of Commerce in Beijing released a survey in which its members complained about new regulations that curb their space. AmCham chairman Ted Dean was quoted at a press conference, saying: "American companies are doing well, and American companies are concerned about in some cases the current regulatory environment and in others the trend line for the regulatory environment."

That's diplomatic language for getting corralled. Jeffrey Immelt, chairman and CEO of GE, was more blunt.

> [A]t a private dinner with fellow businessmen, Immelt criticized China as being hostile to multinational companies and said "I really worry about China. In the end I am not sure they want any of us to win, or to be successful." . . . [L]ast month, Immelt told a group in Shanghai: "I look at my American colleagues, the hardest thing to do in China is get a win-win relationship,"
> —Heidi N. Moore, "GE's Jeff Immelt Says
> It Out Loud About China," *Fortune*, July 2, 2010

However sweet the SAIC-GM relationship may be today, GM's sale of 1 percent of equity to SAIC in 2009 was an ominous event, confirming Chinese control of the Shanghai-GM joint venture. The Shanghai-GM president is from SAIC, and the majority of board members are Chinese. GM finds itself increasingly in the role of a shareholder, not a key driver of the business.

What will happen if relationships at the top of SAIC and GM should for some reason—any reason—turn sour? What will happen when SAIC's own products become globally competitive? Until there is evidence to the contrary, remember Matteo Ricci, his memory palace, and his unfulfilled dreams of Chinese conversion. Then think of GM and other foreign companies as the Matteo Riccis of our era: useful for a time.

In 1989 a senior American executive wrote a confidential memo (featured in Chapter Seven) addressed to the Chrysler board of directors. His conclusion: "For now, we have China on the hook. China needs our parts—we stay in the kit business."

His view was prophetic. For most of the subsequent twenty years, China imported billions of dollars worth of car kits from America, Germany, France, Japan, and Korea.

Imagine that this same veteran executive has resurfaced, this time as special advisor to the U.S. president's special auto task force. He would certainly have a new view on China. The kit-shipping days are over. It's time for fresh thinking. And time for a confidential between-innings wake-up call—something like this:

To: Chairman and Committee Members, U.S. Auto Task Force
From: Special Advisor
Date: August 31, 2011
Subject: Where to from Here?

Some of the information here is tight. I'm not mentioning your names or mine in this document, just in case it finds its way to Wikileaks.

First thing to come to terms with: The global auto industry's power center has shifted to Asia, with China at its heart. Far more vehicles are produced and sold in Asia—some twenty-eight million this year—than in either Europe or America. Asia will remain out front for the next twenty years.

China is strong, very strong. But not invincible. They have some real problems, too.

Costs of materials and people are rising fast. The strategic approach that has carried them so far—labor-intensive products for export—is not going to last.

Home field advantage works only at home. Chinese companies are accustomed to enjoying an edge over foreigners at home, thanks to rules skewed in China's favor. They will have a much more difficult time making overseas investments work—different language, new culture, unfamiliar nuances, a fresh set of rules. Just look at what happened to SAIC with SsangYong.

For the Chinese, jobs are the number one priority. Beijing planners will push their industries to create better-paying jobs at home. Look for China to manufacture and export higher-value goods, including cars.

Within five years, Chinese cars will be coming to our shores. China will need continued access to U.S. consumers. That's where we have some leverage.

China makes regulations part of its competitive arsenal. To give ourselves a fighting chance, we must do the same. To that end, I propose new ground rules:

Rule #1: If the Chinese want to sell their cars to Americans, they must invest in plants in America.

Rule #2: Chinese companies will be free to own 100 percent of their operations in America—*provided* that American car companies get the same rights in China. (If the Chinese refuse, then America will reciprocate. Chinese companies that want to sell in America will be required to joint venture with city or a state government. Have the Chinese start out with the City of Detroit and the UAW as partners.)

Rule #3: Profits from operations stay inside the United States. Repatriation to China will be limited and will require approvals

(*Continued*)

from the U.S. government. That's not an extreme demand—it's just quid pro quo.

OK, that's what the U.S. government can do when the Chinese enter the U.S. market. But businesses must step up, too, when it comes to our ventures in China.

I talk to many foreign executives making good money in China. They tell me that superior technology and exceptional products alone are not enough. What's also essential is a kind of hard tenacity.

American car companies—or any business—should always expect to encounter walls, roadblocks, and other obstructions in China. We must find ways over, under, and around them. Build loyalty among Chinese consumers, while persevering through nasty regulatory surprises and market ambushes.

Staying in the game takes guts and perseverance. And a willingness every day to insist, shout, cajole, demand, push, press, shoulder, and shove your way through to the market.

Competing inside China is just a street fight with a veneer of civility. American companies, no matter what they produced, used to win street fights. Now they've become perhaps too polite. To prevail in China, we need to become a little less congenial and a lot more relentless. Take the punch, get knocked on our asses, stand back up, dust ourselves off, and go at it again.

Nothing less will do.

INDEX